An Awakening Within

An Awakening Within

Stories and Reflections to Rekindle Your Spirit and Awaken Your Soul!

Jeffrey Alan Hall

Writer's Showcase
San Jose New York Lincoln Shanghai

An Awakening Within
Stories and Reflections to Rekindle Your Spirit and Awaken Your Soul!

Writer's Showcase
an imprint of iUniverse, Inc.

For information address:
iUniverse, Inc.
5220 S. 16th St., Suite 200
Lincoln, NE 68512
www.iuniverse.com

ISBN: 0-595-21027-9

Printed in the United States of America

DEDICATION

To my son Joshua. May the roads that I have traveled and the lessons I have learned, gently lead you along the path of light.

CONTENTS

FORWARD

I am excited and honored to have the opportunity to write this forward for my friend Jeffrey Alan Hall. I first came to know Jeffrey through his compelling column in Colorado Serenity Magazine. When each issue arrived I would immediately stop all activity and turn to his pages. His "Higher Ground" column has been a multivitamin for my soul. I find his work clear, spiritual, and poignant—timely and timeless.

I believe the purpose of our lives is to bring forth on earth the expression of our highest good. The human spirit is innately good. It is our soul's responsibility to honor and nurture that spirit in our children. We must devote ourselves to being a catalyst to awaken this greatness within.

In reading Jeffrey's words over the years I have been reminded often that as I look back upon my life, the moments when I have really lived are the moments when I have done things in the spirit of love. Notice for a moment how you feel when you surround yourself, your mind, and soul with true abundance; when you move from being closed to being open. Do you feel more possible? Do you feel more alive?

Martin Luther King Jr. said, "Our goal is to create a beloved community and this will require a qualitative change in our souls as well as a quantitative change in our lives."

As a global community we are being asked to express from our hearts—no less than greatness. In acceptance, compassion, and unconditional love we must take a stand. We need to show up heart first, ready to be a force for good.

In both my clinical and personal experiences I have witnessed the power of thought as one of the most powerful forces in directing one's life.

This force coupled with the most powerful—love—can be a transformational tandem that will empower you to live the life of your dreams. Inspire yourself with the true knowing that even in the darkest night, our spirit's brilliance will illuminate the way. Jeffrey's words are like candles guiding the way on this most auspicious journey.

I encourage you to give yourself fully to the following pages. Let them envelop your thoughts and your heart. Wishing you blessings on your journey.

Dr. James Rouse
Optimum Wellness
KUSA TV
Denver, Colorado

ACKNOWLEDGEMENTS

The completion of a book is seldom the result of one person. This book is no exception. I am ever so grateful to the many wonderful people in my life—*angels*, as I see it—who have given so much of their personal time to make *An Awakening Within* a reality.

First, I would like to thank my publisher, Writers Showcase and all the folks at iUniverse for doing so many things right. A special thanks to Mike Altman for covering all the bases every step of the way.

My friends at Colorado Serenity Magazine have supported my work for many years. A heart felt thanks to Doug Kinzy for taking a risk on an unknown writer and actually paying me to do something I love. Thank you for believing in me!

Dr James Rouse has been my coach and mentor. Your friendship and inspiration will never be taken for granted.

As I write these words, I am struggling to find a way to thank all of the thousands of readers who have given me so much encouragement along the way. You have no idea how uplifting your emails and phone calls have been. Thank you for allowing me to live my dream.

I would also like to thank all of my Life Coaching clients for their never-ending support. It is a privilege to work with all of you toward the accomplishment of your dreams. Thank you for your trust and belief in my work.

I am blessed to have a wonderful family that has provided a source of inspiration for all that I do. Thanks for letting me *hide out* in my study and do what I love to do. And Jan, thank you, my love, for pointing me in the right direction and keeping the vision alive. Here's to another twenty-two years!

Joshua, you are the finest son any man could ask for. Thank you for the lessons you continue to teach me along the path. You brighten my world each and every day. I love you.

There have been so many spiritual masters who have touched my life and led me along the path of light. To Jesus, Buddha, Muhammad, Lao Tzu, Gandhi and all of the great role models ever to walk the earth, thank you for your messages of love and light and for living the potential in all of us.

To Wayne Dyer, Marianne Williamson, Neale Donald Walsch, and Stuart Wilde, thank you for your truth and wisdom. I will forever be a student of your work.

To Helen Schucman and William Thetford, my deepest appreciation for allowing the God force to write *A Course In Miracles* through you. It has changed my life—and the lives of thousands—forever.

Finally, thanks to God—the infinite power within—for co-creating my life on earth and supporting my desires with all the power of the universe.

Introduction

*"You must learn the cost of sleeping and refuse to pay it.
Only then will you decide to awaken"*
—A Course In Miracles

Buddha was once asked, "What are you?"

The question was posed by a large group of his followers, struggling to understand the seemingly *superhuman qualities* of their spiritual master. They had watched in awe, as his mere presence could restore sight to the blind, hearing to the deaf and generate countless other miracles of a magnitude reserved only for the gods.

Even the powerful—kings and other royalty—bowed at his feet and worshiped him in the same way that Jesus would be worshipped centuries later. Certainly, he could not be a mere mortal man for no mere mortal could command the powers of the universe with such confidence and grace. But if he was not a man then what was he?

"Are you a god?" they asked.

"No," he replied.

"Well, then you must be a saint?"

"No, I am not."

"Are you an angel or someone sent from above?"

"No" he insisted.

"Then, *what are you?*" they demanded.

Buddha answered, "I am awake."

Buddha had come to understand and *awaken to* the power that lives within each of us—the power of love. He had surrendered his ego—the part of us that often blocks our ability to embrace the spiritual—and allowed *love and only love* to guide his earthly experience. He had awakened to the power of God—the power of love—not by looking outside of himself, but by looking within. Just like Jesus and all other spiritual masters, he had transcended his human limitations by embracing his spiritual power.

I call this power *the God force*, for its energy flows through everything that we have come to know as our *reality*. God created the universe with this *power of love* and that same energy allows us to co-create with God, the life of our choosing. By surrendering to this power we truly *awaken*, for suddenly we open our eyes and *wake up* to a new understanding of what it means to be alive. In a *holy instant*, we begin to see life and all its possibilities, as we have never seen it before.

To *awaken* to this power is to become aware. Aware of the so-called coincidences of life and to know that they are not coincidences at all, but rather lessons that our souls have come to earth to learn or to teach. Each lesson takes us further along the path of light, opening yet another door and *awakening* yet another dimension of our souls. With each lesson learned or taught, the path of light gets brighter and our eyes open more widely. Where once we were blind, now we can see.

Each story and reflection on the pages that follow, represent some of the many *awakenings—the lessons*—my soul has experienced while traveling along the path of light. The life changing moments that have allowed me to move further towards my truth, reduce the endless chatter of my ego and surrender to the power of love.

Some of these stories may feel familiar to you; for I am certain that in many cases, your soul has come to earth to learn or to teach the same lessons as mine. If so, that particular story will ring true for you as you recognize our parallel paths. Smile and enjoy it! Bask in the glory of how similar, yet different, our life experiences can be.

I think you will find God's fingerprints—like a child eating chocolate on a hot afternoon—visibly imprinted on every page. As I would rise in the morning to meditate and pray, I would ask God for the words I was to write that day. The response was often immediate and as soon as my fingers hit the key-board the words would flow with an easy cadence and rhythm. During these moments, I was but an instrument in God's hands, not knowing exactly how the story would begin or end. As always, I simply surrendered to the God force and placed my trust in a universe that knows exactly what Its doing.

At other times, the words might elude me for days, only to *show up* at the most unforeseen moments as I was out-and-about experiencing *this thing called life.* Just as I was becoming a little impatient, thinking that perhaps I had writers block, once again the universe would deliver just the right words at just the right time. I simply had to pay attention and be prepared to receive them no matter when or where they arrived.

Frequently, I would come upon a verse or a group of words some-where—in the Bible, the Koran, the Tao, the Bhagavad-Gita, the Dhammapada, the Tao-te Ching or A Course in Miracles—and know that what I had just read was not an accident. In those instances, the ideas expressed within those sacred teachings formed the conceptual framework of that particular story.

My writing does not draw from any one religion or belief system, but rather takes a holistic approach to spirituality. I believe in a spiritual tapestry that incorporates the teachings from *all spiritual masters*—those who lived thousands of years ago, those who lived hundreds of years ago and those who live today. I am compelled to take this approach because after four decades of walking the spirit trail, I am convinced of at least two things: God has no reli-gion and God doesn't just speak to some of us, God speaks to us all.

Like spokes in a wheel with God at the center, we are all coming from different directions but headed towards the same destination. It makes no difference how you choose to connect to the God force, only that you do. Since God is not separate from us but rather lives inside each of us, the ways we choose to connect to this power will be as different and as unique as we are. Every path to God is worth taking because every path to God has something to teach us.

In many ways, this book represents my hope for a better tomorrow. A tomorrow built upon the solid foundation of love as opposed to the shifting sands of fear. There is optimism in my heart that bridges can be built to span the distance between us and allow us to understand each other as never before. I am confident that somehow we can eliminate the hatred and war that seeks to destroy the future of our children and replace it with a lasting peace and heaven on earth. The time to awaken our souls is now, for the cost of sleeping has become far too high a price to pay.

If there is to be an awakening, it must be with in us—within each of our souls—for that is the only place that true and lasting change can occur. We must awaken to the wonderful possibilities of what we can become as one world, and not focus on what we have been as separate nations. We must awaken to the things we are for—the things that unite us as a planet—and not dwell on what we are against by drawing lines in the sand. We must awaken to the power of the God force and allow it to lead our collective consciousness to a new and higher way of being. We must awaken to the power of love.

I look forward to a day when if asked, "What are you?" we will not respond by saying, we are Christian or Muslim, or Buddhist or Jew. We will not even consider suggesting that we are American or Russian or Chinese or Arabic. We will not see ourselves as white or black or yellow or red. That somehow, we will transcend our differences and begin to recognize our brothers and sisters in the eyes of every human being.

I continue to pray for the day when we will see ourselves as members of the same family of man *connected by love* to the same God. I continue to pray for the day when all barriers are removed, all fear eliminated, all differences tolerated. I look forward to a time when if asked, "What are you?" each and every man, woman and child on this magnificent blue planet, will join hands with one another and answer, "We are awake."

Jeffrey Alan Hall
Evergreen, Colorado
November 2001

GIFTS OF THE ANGELS

"We will treasure the wisdom that has been laid at our feet, by those who have traveled before us. We will surrender with honesty, courage and grace and trust in the power of Spirit. We will drink of its sweetness and taste of its truth with the wonder and innocence of children. We will acknowledge our place in the circle of life and breathe deep the gifts of the angels."
Jeffrey Alan Hall

All Tommy ever wanted was to meet his hero face to face. To look into the eyes of the man who had hit more home runs than any other mortal. But now, with his eight year-old body ravaged by the effects of cancer, Tommy had been given but a few days to live. Clinging to life with every labored breath, the young boy held fast to his dream. But time was running out. His destiny with *The Babe* was not to be. Or was it?

As the sun rose the next morning on the day that would become Tommy's last, a man appeared claiming to be Babe Ruth's agent. Bearing autographed pictures of the legendary slugger and a bat that he said the Babe *wanted Tommy to have*, the unknown man gave Tommy the gift of a lifetime. Tears flowed from the eyes of everyone in the room as Tommy kissed the picture, held tightly to the bat, closed his eyes, and died—with a smile on his face.

No one is exactly sure what happened in the moments that followed. But somehow, in the flourish of activity, as Tommy's mother held the lifeless body of her son and relatives and friends said their final good-byes, the man who had given Tommy *so much* seemed to disappear. By all accounts, he was a stranger—never before seen and never to be seen again. The so-called *agent* of Babe Ruth walked back into the world with humility and grace. He accomplished what he had set out to do. He had improved the life of another.

Scenes like this happen everyday in many different ways. Someone reaches out to offer the gift of hope, the gift of love, or the gift of compassion. Someone *cares enough to care enough* and extends a hand to another. Each link in the chain is completed one after the other by *angels in disguise*—common people with uncommon courage who go about the business of helping others with little fanfare or recognition. They are a gift from Spirit and they are everywhere...

There are angels among us. Those with illuminated eyes, who stand at the crossroads of life and lift us up to heights unknown. We will know them by the childlike innocence that radiates from their souls, by the way their truth and ours so nicely intertwine. In the presence of their being we become alive and more fully engaged in the process of finding our path. They never ask us to trade our beliefs for theirs, never demand that we become something we are not. For they seem to honor the truth in everyone while at the same time holding their own beliefs deeply within. They encourage us to take a *leap of faith*, to believe in ourselves, and trust in the voice that whispers, "You can do it!"

Angels make us feel comfortable. Even if we've only known them for a short time, we feel as if we've known them forever. There is no need for clever conversation, no need to tread lightly. We feel compelled to just *be ourselves*, let our hearts fall a little further down our sleeves and express our truth with honesty and love. They accept us just as we are and never attempt to manipulate us with guilt or some self-proclaimed authority. We freely *show them our scars* without reservation and in turn they show us theirs. We trust them and know that they have our best interest at heart.

Angels gently remind us to *live in the present* when backward glances cloud our judgment and we are tempted to look over our shoulder at the past or race into the future. Angels tell us to simply relax, slow down to the speed of life and enjoy the process of *becoming*. They encourage us to control our thoughts, to be still, to embrace the silence and to just *be*.

Angels will often lead us inside ourselves for answers, to remember our own truth and courageously manifest our destiny. And as we step inside the magical kingdom of our souls, the windows to enlightenment begin to swing open and we are welcomed inside with open arms. It is through these windows that we will begin to treasure the wisdom that has been laid at our feet, by those who have traveled before us. We will surrender with honesty, courage and grace and trust in the power of Spirit. We will drink of its sweetness and taste of its truth with the wonder and innocence of children. We will acknowledge our place in the circle of life and breathe deep the gifts of the angels.

Many spiritual masters have attempted to describe the angelic experience, but I believe Jesus said it best: *We are in this world but not of this world*. We are indeed angels—spiritual beings—experiencing a physical existence. We have come from the Universal power of Spirit and we shall return to that same Power when the life force that runs through our veins returns to dust. There are those who will lead us and those who will teach us every step of the way. They are angels. They have come bearing gifts. And they are no further away than the proof of our own existence, for we are them and they are us.

As we move along our individual paths, we must take caution to live our own truth. But that doesn't mean we must do it alone. I have come to understand that there are many who are on this earth *to help and encourage us* along the path of light. I call them angels in disguise—spiritual wizards—soul mates with whom we connect with at the deepest levels. You know the people I'm talking about—those kindred spirits with whom, in their presence, you feel at home. These same people are the *guiding lights* who direct us on our journey and seem to have an uncanny sense and knowledge of exactly where they are going. Compass in hand, they point the way to Spirit. They know the way because, just like all of us, they've been there before. The difference is, they've chosen to *remember*.

The people that brighten up our lives, those that offer a helping hand, honor our dreams, believe in our abilities and encourage us to become our highest gift, *show up in our lives* at just the right time and in just the right place. It is *not a mere coincidence* that they are here, but rather a divine intervention of the most cosmic kind. Metaphysical? Perhaps. But from womb to tomb and beyond, those who are *in this world but not of this world* stand ready *to* direct us towards the light. They are here and among us all the days of our eternal lives.

Each of us is an *angel in waiting*. Each of us can lift another human being to higher levels of existence through our ability to let go of our egos and focus instead on understanding the needs of another. By giving of ourselves, our time, our money—whatever gifts we have been given—we can improve the world *one person at a time*. Our mission doesn't have to be grand in scale but rather simply *doing small things in a grand way*. We were all sent *to teach and be taught*, to discover the lessons that will free us of our self-inflicted traumas and man-made guilt. Angels draw our focus away from ourselves and ask us to reach out, to get involved, and to make things happen. *For it is in healing the lives of others that we begin to heal ourselves.*

I am reminded of a woman I once knew who after years of seeing her best friend battle depression, simply suggested that she take a few moments everyday to send thank-you notes to anyone and everyone who had helped her—in any way—during the previous twenty-four hours. Upon taking her advice, her friend's depression began to subside as she came to understand how many people actually cared for her. Everyday she would go through an entire box of thank-you notes! The experience was overwhelming.

Then there was an old friend of mine who decided to give up his Sunday mornings to join other similar souls in mowing the lawns of the elderly within his community. He didn't have to do those things, but by focusing on the needs of others, by becoming more angelic in his dealings with those in need, he improved the quality of his own life. His life took on a whole new meaning, deep inside, where it really counts. I will never forget how surprised he was when, out of nowhere, fresh baked pies and picnic baskets filled with home made goodies began to show up at his doorstep. By giving love away he had invited love into his life.

Our world is the bi-product of an accumulation of angelic gifts. Since the beginning of mankind, people have been helping people, and in doing so have created a better world; generation after generation. The everyday things that we so often take for granted represent the cumulative efforts of so many wonderful people—angels in their day—who sacrificed personal gain for the betterment of mankind. Yes there has been war, yes there has been famine—yes there have been a million ugly blisters that have tarnished the soul of the world—but there has also been Mother Teresa, Martin Luther King and Gandhi. Yes, hatred still exists in every corner of the earth, *but so does love and in much greater supply than many would have us believe.* Somehow, through all of the evil that the nightly news continues to drum into our heads, *fear continues to give-way to love* and goodness finds a way to prevail.

It has been said that the world would end tomorrow if it were not for the collective prayers of millions of people—angels—who continue to ask the Universe for peace, love and understanding. Angels have been on their knees since the beginning of time, providing the spiritual glue that keeps everything together. The Universe speaks through them and they in turn *listen to* and respond to its call. None of these people are special or more gifted or somehow better connected to Spirit. Rather, these are simply people who *never give up* in their desire to make the world a better place.

These are the souls who *dedicate their lives* to worthy causes. Some are *spiritreneurs* who start businesses that not only make money but also make a difference. Others spend their lives finding a cure for a deadly disease or comforting the sick or feeding the hungry.

They are our teachers, our poets, our dancers and our young. They are our mothers, our fathers, our artists and our old. They work in the fields of medicine and in the wheat fields of Kansas. They create our music and grow our food. They can be found in a million different places doing a million different things, *all in the name of love*. They are the passionate ones who *care enough to care enough*. Are you one of them? Am I?

Becoming an angel doesn't require much training. You don't have to quit your current job, take a class or earn a graduate degree. You can begin right where you are, right now. All you need to do is ask yourself one simple question: *How can I use the gifts that I have been given to improve the life of another?* Only *you* know the answer, only *you* can ask the question.

Somewhere, someplace—at this very moment—another human being is in desperate need of an angel. They might be at the end of their rope or the end of their life. They may need to meet their hero, hear a word of encouragement or simply be on the receiving end of a hug. They may be across town, across the country or across the room. Open the eyes of your heart; invite them in. Be an angel in disguise and offer up your gifts to anyone in need. Help to heal the wounds of another and don't be surprised when in your time of need, others do the same for you.

Don't be too busy to give or too proud to receive. Acknowledge *your* place in the circle of life and breathe deep the gifts of the angels.

Some Things To Consider

Have you been an angel to anyone lately? List at least five angelic things you've done for others in the past year. Is there anyone that needs you to be an angel now? List at least five angelic things you plan to do for others in the next six months. Do them.

OLD HIPPIES, NEW CAUSES AND THE RETURN OF THE LAVA LAMP

"If you have built castles in the air, your work need not be lost;
that is where they should be. Now put the foundations under them."
Henry David Thoreau

I saw the mother and her son from a distance. He was probably four or maybe five years of age, straw-like blonde hair poking out from underneath a baseball cap, a smile from cheek to cheek. He was running full-tilt in his Oshkosh overalls, past the oak trees that line Cedar Street. Carefree and confident, he was having a blast! Mom was laughing and exclaiming how fast he was and how someday he might grow up to be a famous athlete. It felt like happily ever after. Like black and white television. Like a white picket fence. Like Mayberry.

But then I began to wonder how long it might last, this childhood innocence, this thinking that *anything could be done*. How soon before he would head off to school, to *the real world,* where adults with good intentions, would set him upon the lathe of life and begin to shape and bend him into conformity; forced to learn the *ways of the world*—the world you and I live in.

I feel sorry for the children. For it seems they only get about five good years of living fully in the present moment, before the ways of the world begin to aggressively reel them in. Like a young marlin fighting to break away and escape capture, they pull hard against the line, until finally, unable to pull any longer, they succumb to the pressure. The challenge to their freedom came and went and like a wild horse, they were broken.

The same challenge came for many of us baby boomers just after John, Paul, George and Ringo came on the scene. But luckily for some of us, before the lathe could snag us—before the screws could be tightened—we rose to the occasion, pounded on our chests and stood up against the establishment. Just to prove our point, we grew our hair long and adopted a radical dress code—blue jeans, sandals and t-shirts. Let's face it, back then earrings or body piercing would have landed us in the loony bin or worse. Tattoos? Forget it. They were only for sailors.

So our hair became our badge of honor. Beautiful locks, long and flowing—symbolic of our indifference to a culture seemingly gone mad and definitely a unique way of setting ourselves apart from the mainstream. It also pissed off every adult within viewing distance. That of course would never happen today. By today's standards, our looks would have been considered mainstream or even conservative, but back then, baby, we were radical! Don't let anybody tell *us* to conform. We were going to stand our ground, change the world and make a difference! I'm "talkin' bout my generation" here!

But the decades rolled by and our acne cleared up. Everyone except Dick Clark got older. We began to drop our guard instead of acid, get real jobs and become just like *them*. Some of us learned the art of "Dressing For Success," of tying neckties or shining our wingtip shoes, while others figured out how to manipulate the system and buy the big mansion on the hill. By the time we rolled into the eighties we were worshiping "Reaganomics" and becoming virtual clones of our mothers and fathers—more obsessed with stock portfolios and BMW's than with the issues of the world. "Forget feeding the homeless," we declared, "where are we going for sushi tonight?" Heaven help us, for we did not know what we were doing.

For those of us who took it seriously, there was supposed to have been a significant change in the world sometime before Nixon lied to us and just after Marilyn sang Happy Birthday Mr. President. There was supposed to have been a radical shift in the way we viewed life and love and politics. The change was all about rock and roll and braless women. About free speech, loud music and Fender guitars. We played our records backwards and waited for a sign from the Walrus. We believed in love and peace and passive resistance. We were hippies. We wanted to make love not war.

Somewhere near Woodstock in upstate New York, on a farm in the middle of nowhere, peace was supposed to plant a seed that would grow into a beanstalk and lead us to the path of light. On one solitary weekend in a muddy cornfield, we caught a brief glimpse of the "Wizard of OZ" and it was ours for the taking. But instead of following the yellow brick road, we looked up at mom's bronze silhouette as she stood in New York harbor, took off our baseball caps, and let the lathe of life steal our dream. Mom kept holding the torch but we let the fire go out. Plain and simple; we freaked out. Lennon's "Imagine" faded away. Manson's "Helter-Skelter" was off and running.

The clock was ticking as those of us in bell-bottoms and tie-dyes fought the good fight. We taped and bandaged the wounded, regrouped and took another run at it. But regardless of who started the fire, we couldn't find a way to put it out. Maybe the drugs finally took their toll or maybe we just got tired of pushing against the wind. Maybe it ended with the death of Janis or Hendrix or Morrison. Maybe Watergate made us so sick all we wanted to do was go home and have a good cry. Whatever it was, we all retreated to our chambers while the dream died a slow and painful death. Then along came disco and well...I'll save that for another story.

Nowadays it seems that, not unlike our parents, many of us simply go through the motions of life instead of really living it. The idea of turning out like Ozzie and Harriet may have scared us to death when we were younger but have you looked in the mirror lately? Now that we are in positions of power, and actually running America, we seem to have given up on the notion that we can make a difference. Let me get this straight: When we were young and had no power we thought we could change the world. Now that we have the power we would rather sit on the couch and watch our big screen TV's. In the words of Pink Floyd, we have indeed become "comfortably numb." Prozac has never been more *en vogue*. If we ever actually "checked in to see what condition our condition was in" we would pronounce the victim dead.

Remember when some of us were proud to stand up and be counted, like the Chinese boy who stood face to face with that tank in Tienamen Square just a decade ago or the kids who were shot and killed at Kent State by Nixon's tin soldiers? We despised complacency. We wanted the truth. We would stop at nothing to get it.

In the days of *our generation* there was something in the air, other than pot, that convinced us "all we needed was love." I think we were on to something—something big! As the spiritual tide has begun to return in America, as a relationship with God has become increasingly more important to many of us, I believe that back in the "old days" we may have been more than just a *little bit* right.

When I look around today, I see a million causes and organizations crying out for volunteers, hungry for boomers just like you and me to step in, roll up our sleeves and believe enough to make a difference. I see so many striking similarities between the passion these groups have for their causes and the passion we had for ours that I can't imagine why more of us don't get involved.

Jefferson Airplane's "Volunteers of America" has never been more relevant. The issues we felt so strongly about back then are resurfacing under different names today. Activists are still needed. Only this time, because of our socio-economic position, we are better suited to affect change and make things happen than ever before. You don't need to grow your hair long (even if you still had some) or drop acid to make a statement. Just go to work on improving our world right where you are, right now.

But what about love and peace you ask? Can we still include that in the mix? Absolutely. There's a spiritual renaissance taking place all over the world. No one is confining themselves to a bed in Montreal but people of all walks of life are connecting or reconnecting to love and spirit and God in record numbers throughout the world. Prayer and meditation are making a big come back as alternative forms of medical treatment. Suddenly the postmodern world is focused on improving the health of the soul. It truly is time to get ready, for the train is coming. Now, as in the past—you don't need a ticket to get on board.

I'll make you a deal: Take just one day a month, thumb your nose at the establishment and do something really radical—take a day off from work! Get involved in your community, your church or synagogue. Become a big brother, drive the elderly to the grocery store or work at a homeless shelter. If after 3 months of doing so, you don't feel absolutely wonderful and just a little like you did when you had more hair, less wrinkles and a lot less concern for what people think, then I will personally buy you a lava lamp. I'm serious—a brand spanking new one! Just like passion and commitment and courage, they're suddenly back in style.

Some Things To Consider

Try and remember that magical time in your life—we all have one—when you felt you could do and be anything your heart desired. Now ask yourself, what happened to that passion? Where did the fire go? If you look deeply enough within, you will find that there's still a few embers glowing. Recapture that feeling, reposition it towards a new cause or goal and get going! Time is of the essence.

An Awakening Within

"Today, I will begin to create my life exactly the way I choose it to be, know-ing that the power to become is limited only by my thoughts. I will use prayer and meditation to manifest my own destiny and bring into my life only those people and things that will further develop and enrich the path I have chosen. I will remove myself from toxic relationships and move closer to those souls who walk the path of light."

Jeffrey Alan Hall

Emily was dying of breast cancer. Diagnosed at the young age of 31, she had battled the disease with the usual arsenal of drugs and radiation. Now frail and weakened by weeks of chemotherapy, she stood in disbelief as her doctors told her there was "nothing more they could do." Emily was given six weeks to live and sent home to die.

"Looking back on the last few months," she remarked just days after dismissal from the hospital, "I realize had it not been for this disease, I would have never taken the time to find my spiritual self. In some ways, the cancer saved my life."

"What do you mean "saved your life?" My God, Emily, you're dying of cancer. I can't bear the thought that soon you may be gone. How can you look at this in such a positive light?"

"It's true that at the moment my body is dying," she whispered, wrap-ping her arms around me for the emotional comfort only touch can pro-vide. "But, you know, years ago, long before the cancer, my soul was slowly dying. It just shriveled up and began to starve from lack of attention. On the outside I looked great, but on the inside I was spiritually dead. The toughest part was that no one knew it. No one but me."

"But now," she continued with the excitement of a child, "now I feel as if I have been given a new set of eyes. For the first time, I am beginning to see and appreciate the many treasures of life—the things I always took for granted, the presence of God. The doctors may have written me off, but God hasn't given up on me yet. I am praying for a miracle: to be *healed* by the power of God. I know that my prayers will be heard."

Emily reached deep inside the pocket of her faded jeans and pulled out a tattered piece of paper. "Here," she said. "Read this. This is how I intend to live my life for whatever time I have left."

I could no longer contain my tears as I read the heartfelt words that Emily had written. At that moment I realized that, even as death lay on her doorstep, when it would have been justifiable for her to be angry, bitter or just plain mad at the world, this beautiful soul had chosen to embrace life and the power of God in a way that few of us ever do. The words read:

"Today, I will begin to acknowledge the truth that lives in my soul and the kindred spirit of love and honesty that permeates my heart and speaks through my feelings. Today, I will take a step towards remembering the childlike innocence that accompanied me on my journey from the womb, an innocence that I allowed to die a slow and painful death.

I will believe in the power of God, knowing with certainty that God is living in the very depths of my soul. I will allow God's presence to be expressed through the words of my lips and the work of my hands. "How can I help?" will be the greeting I will bestow upon everyone I meet.

I will listen to the little voice that speaks to my heart, knowing that it is the voice of truth, love and spirit. By making still the world around me, I will truly listen with new-found ears to the message that is written in the wind. In these moments of silence, I will notice and pay attention to the beauty that surrounds me, as if I am seeing the colors of life for the first time.

Not only will I love every living thing with unbridled passion, but I will first love myself with unconditional forgiveness of my past mistakes. As long as God allows my soul to occupy this bodily vessel, I will live in the present moment, focused on helping all of mankind with the unique gifts that have been bestowed upon me. Guilt no longer has a place in my vocabulary.

Today, I will begin to create my life exactly the way I choose it to be, knowing that the power to become is limited only by my thoughts. I will use prayer and meditation to manifest my own destiny and bring into my life only those people and things that will further develop and enrich the path I have chosen. I will remove myself from toxic relationships and move closer to those souls who walk the path of light.

Today, I will remove the shackles that have held my spirit in check, allowing others to do the same as they seek their own path, in their own way and at their own speed. I will offer forgiveness to everyone and everything and, in doing so, will find freedom—freedom to love, freedom to live and freedom to courageously direct my earthly existence with the spiritual powers of my soul. Let the music begin!"

Many of us are blessed with good physical health but are spiritually undernourished. *An Awakening Within* can happen to all of us if we will only create enough silence in our lives to tune in to the power of God. A terminal disease is not required, but we must act now. For in truth, our physical life on earth *is* terminal, and the opportunity to contribute to a better world is as fleeting as the ticking of a clock.

Some Things To Consider

What would you do differently if you knew you only had six months to live? Why aren't you doing it? Take some time today to meditate and connect to Spirit. Listen to the voice within and begin to follow your hearts desire. How can you take a few baby steps toward your dreams today?

LOVE THE ONE YOU'RE WITH

"Our deepest fear is not that we are inadequate. Our deepest fear is that we are powerful beyond measure. It is our light, not our darkness, that most frightens us. We ask ourselves, who am I to be brilliant, gorgeous, talented and fabulous? Actually, who are you not to be? You are a child of God. Your playing small does not serve the world. There's nothing enlightened about shrinking so that other people won't feel insecure around you."

Marianne Williamson

While running on the beautiful island of Kauai recently, I spotted a local artist diligently working on a sand sculpture. I was so taken by her uncommon use of detail that I departed from my normal policy of *never stop for anything* and paused just long enough to take in the full breadth of her work. I was awe struck. It was truly the work of a master.

"How do you come up with such beautiful art," I asked.

"Let me answer that question with a new twist on the words of Michelangelo," she replied. "The sculpture already lies within the pile of sand. My job is to simply remove the excess sand that surrounds the creation. God already created the sculpture. It's already perfect and complete. I just let its light shine."

So it is with life, I thought. Each of us is born perfect and complete. We are God's creation. We need only love the one we're with—ourselves—for who and what we are. Yet, how many of us understand this? Instead, we seem to fear our true power—a power that was given to us by the Creator for the purpose of manifesting our own destiny. The greater our fear, the more time we waste trying to improve what was already perfect on the day

we were born. We falsely place our faith in others, on things outside ourselves, instead of seeking the answers where they truly lie—within our
own hearts. Our truth gets buried under a mound of sand.

We humans have the distinction of being the only species on the planet
that, depending on our mood, may or may not choose to love ourselves.
Ever known a squirrel that didn't like himself and wished he were a cat?
Or, how about a cow with such low self esteem that he committed suicide.
But here's the funny part—whether we choose to love ourselves as perfect
creations, designed in God's image or see ourselves as dirty rotten
scoundrels, we're right. The choice is ours and will ultimately determine
our destiny. As we think, so we become.

Loving ourselves can at first seem, well, a little difficult. Many of us
were raised in religious households (I said religious, not spiritual—big difference!) where we were taught that we humans are flawed individuals created in sin. That somehow we are not worthy of love from anyone
including ourselves.

But, it seems to me, that to love ourselves—to be comfortable with
who we are—is to understand that we were created in love not sin. God is
love and since He created us, we too are love. In the eyes of the universe,
you have nothing to prove. From womb to tomb and beyond, you are perfect just being you, just the way you are. Can you imagine how different
the world would be if we all understood this? What would we need to
own? Why would we ever go to war? Who would we need to impress?

Whenever we are unable to love ourselves or someone else, we have
likely allowed fear to replace love as the driving force in our lives. As time
goes on, we allow all of our decisions to be based on fear. After a while, we
forget what love really feels like. We spend so much time in a fearful state
that fear becomes our only motivation. We want to love ourselves but the
fear of our own power frightens us. So we distance ourselves from our true
desires and believe that somehow we are unworthy. Fear wins and love
loses. We hand over our power to someone else.

Jesus, Buddha and other enlightened masters were different from the rest of us in one important way—love was all they knew. Every decision they made, every action they took was based on love not fear. Love was the truth that set them free because love eliminated fear from every facet of their lives. With fear removed, they were free to love themselves and others at the level that God intended. Because love rather than fear drove them, they were able to accomplish great things—things that we are all capable of doing once we learn to remove fear and love ourselves. Jesus himself said that we would do everything He did and more. Few of us took Him seriously. Perhaps more of us should.

Fear is very easy to spot. It can be seen when we choose to judge others instead of extending compassion. It can be found in disrespect, intolerance and insensitivity. Whenever we attempt to be understood before we attempt to understand, we are acting out of fear. Most of the world runs on fear. If you've ever watched the nightly news, you know what I mean. If fear were replaced with love, most, if not all of the world's problems would be solved. Hatred, the result of fear, dies when love prevails.

Love of self is a direct reflection of our ability to set fear aside, forgive and surrender. We must learn to trust the force that moves the universe and take our hands off the handlebars. The result is faith. Faith in ourselves and faith in others ultimately leads to a state of bliss that eliminates fear and keeps us on the path of light. When we surrender, we say to the universe "I trust you." It is in our trusting that we are able to manifest our destiny and become our highest gift.

By trusting the universe and suspending our need to judge, we are able to forgive both ourselves and others. We learn that everything, including ourselves, is just as it is suppose to be. We begin to understand that the universe does not make mistakes.

For thousands of years, God heard our prayers for a better world and He sent help. He sent you. Take it seriously. Learn to love yourself and allow your unique light to illuminate the darkest corners of the world. Don't fear your own power; embrace it.

Jesus said, "Love your neighbor as yourself." The underlying assumption here is that we must first love ourselves—a lot! After all, if we hated ourselves and then loved our neighbors in the same way, what good would that do? They would only retaliate and hate us back. The next thing you know, they would hire a Realtor, put their house on the market and just move away.

Some Things To Consider

How often do you let your light shine? Are you playing small in the arena of life or living up to your highest gift—your full potential? Are there things about yourself that you just don't like? Why? Learn to embrace your godliness and love yourself; for it is within yourself that God can be found.

Pamper yourself with kindness. Go get a massage. If you can afford to, get one every week!

Too Much Stuff!

"Sergeant O'Leary is walkin' the beat, at night he becomes a bartender.
He works at Mr. Cacciatore's down on Sullivan Street, across from the medical center.
He's tradin' in his Chevy for a Cadillac, you oughta know by now.
And if he can't drive with a broken back, at least he can polish the fenders.
But it seems such a waste of time, if that's what it's all about.
If that's movin' up then I'm movin' out."

Billy Joel

A friend of mine had everything—I mean absolutely everything! Look up "everything" in the dictionary and there you would find his face—both of them—his original one and the new one, post facelift—the facelift he just had to have at a cost of $8500. He had several cars, three motorcycles, an amazing wardrobe—countless slacks, shirts, shoes, ties, jackets, suites, you name it—an awesome jewelry collection, two homes, three computers, four cell phones, six—count 'em—six electric razors and an entire four-car garage full of a gazillion other things—most of which I never actually saw because it was all buried under a ton of other stuff.

You would think these things would have made him a happy man but in reality he was the most miserable person I have ever known. Why? Because he didn't really own those things but, rather, his things owned him. I knew it, the bank knew it, his credit card company (all six of them) knew it and his fourth wife knew it! He had traded the last twenty years of his life for all of this stuff. He lived his life under a mountain of debt, struggling to pay his bills and missing out on true happiness because of all the things he just had to have—just couldn't live without—and hey, they were on sale!

Like any animal caught in a trap, he struggled to break free but never quite could. The tireless pursuit of happiness through the acquisition of things took over my friend's life and his health began to deteriorate. He began developing a whole host of medical problems, mostly associated with the stress that came from being forced to work at a job he hated because he had to have the high paying job in order to pay for all the stuff he thought he needed. Stuff that I'm sure he thought would ultimately make him happy. More than anyone I ever knew, Bill lived by the motto, "The one with the most stuff when he dies wins!"

Late last August, Bill's participation in the "most stuff contest" ended when he suddenly died from a massive heart attack at the ripe old age of 42. Wanna know the funny part? No one showed up with a plaque or a trophy or a "most stuff award" of any kind. There was no first-place prize, no sweepstakes van in the driveway, no mention on the nightly news about all the stuff Bill had accumulated in his short lifetime. In the end, Bill's stuff meant nothing to anyone but Bill.

We all know people like this—right? Maybe you're one of them? The folks who rush right out and buy something they just saw on TV—the folks who honestly fall for the notion that Madison Avenue knows what is best for them. People who have to own the latest gizmo and gadget—people who believe that happiness lies outside themselves in the accumulation of things. Just like my friend Bill, they sacrifice their time, their relationships, and eventually their lives, in pursuit of that one elusive material possession—that one special thing that will finally make them happy. But happiness is never found in things. Happiness is only found within our hearts. We already own it. It's free!

For us baby boomers, the "I've got to have that thing" brainwashing began when we were just kids. Those of us born in the twenty years after WWII grew up believing that we could and should have everything. After all, we deserved it, right? America had just won the war, we were the strongest nation on earth and everyone who wanted a job had one (or two, depending on how much stuff you wanted)—it was a time to let the *good times* roll. And roll we did!

During the hey-day of the 1950's and 60's, *unbridled consumerism coupled with mass marketing* set out to convince us that acquiring *things* was good—the foundation of the American dream. "Buy this, that, or the other thing," the advertising exclaimed, and "you will be truly happy!"

But just like the cigarettes that the same generation of marketers tried to tell us were safe (the Marlboro Man died of lung cancer), some of us are now beginning to see through this facade and understand that happiness and the acquisition of things are often *mutually exclusive*. We have begun to simplify our lives, step back from the rat race and get a grip on what is really important—family and friends, mind, body and spirit. But others of us haven't changed at all. We are still trying to find happiness the same old way—in a new car, the latest styles, another toy, another this, another that. Let's face it; old habits are hard to break. But break them we must.

I was in Kansas City last week on a business trip, driving down the highway and minding my own business, when I was suddenly bombarded by advertising's number one grassroots weapon in the battle for your wallet—signs. Big signs, small signs, billboards, neon, you name it—hundreds, if not thousands of businesses screaming at me, begging me to spend my money on stuff—their stuff! Stuff I probably don't need, stuff I could definitely live without; stuff that will no doubt be discarded in a few weeks or months or years, only to be replaced by more stuff. The stuff cycle is endless! But we just keep pledging our monetary allegiance—buying more stuff and thinking it will make us happy.

Warning: Doing the same things but expecting a different outcome is the definition of insanity!

Then there's the whole maintenance issue. How much of your time is spent guarding and maintaining your stuff? Think about it. When the weekend rolls around, how much of your free time—the time you spend away from your employer—the time when you get to do the things *you* want to do—gets eaten up by material possessions that need to be cleaned, polished, added on to, painted, repaired, protected, replaced and just plain taken care of. We've become *babysitters* of things. Enough is enough! But will you know when you have *enough*?

Do you really enjoy this process or would you rather be doing something more important with your time? You do understand that you are trading your time (in the form of work) for all your stuff, right? Are you OK with that? At the end of a hard day, as you drag your tired bones into bed, do you look around at all your stuff and genuinely feel fulfilled? Do you honestly feel that giving up your time for these things was a good trade off? Or is there something that (as the bumper sticker says) you'd "rather be doing." Do you own your stuff or does it own you?

Many of us develop our sense of identity from our stuff. We begin to think that we *are* our home, our car, our clothes, our job, our *whatever*. But what happens to our identity if those *things* are suddenly taken away? Does our identity—our sense of who we are—go with them? I think not. Stuff is just stuff—it has no meaning except for the meaning we attach to it. You can *never find meaning among the meaningless*. Yet, many of us spend entire lifetimes trying to do just that.

Your true identity has nothing to with material things. Your true identity is spiritual and was given to you by God the moment you were born. You don't need to—and frankly, you can't—buy it! Happiness doesn't lie outside ourselves in some material object; it lies within our hearts. Can you imagine God looking down and saying, "If only these humans would go out and buy the right stuff. Then, maybe, they would finally understand the true meaning of life." Not the God I know!

Here's a good question: How much of your stuff do you really need? Or better yet, how much are you willing to get rid of? Much has been written these days about *simplifying* our lives and many people are beginning to understand that the first step towards a simpler lifestyle lies in the reduction of the number of things that clutter up our closets, garages, offices and most importantly, our minds. Stuff takes up space and time and energy, which only complicates and distorts our earthly existence. Stuff stresses us out and often forces us to work our whole lives at jobs we hate just to pay for all the stuff we have. A simpler life means less stuff and less stuff means more freedom because when you no longer *need* things to make you happy you are suddenly free to find true happiness—the kind of happiness that lives inside of you and is found in *experiences* not things.

Our love affair with our stuff is very one-sided *because our stuff can't love us back*. Ever try to hug your big screen TV? Try it—it won't respond! You could even look it right in the eye (or the screen) right after a major sporting event (an orgasmic experience for some people) and ask, "Was it as good for you as it was for me?" Trust me, the TV won't give you a sexy hug and light up a cigarette! Nope. When you choose to worship things you're on your own—it's a solitary experience—mental masturbation of the worst kind!

And let's face it—you never really own your stuff, anyway. You don't really own your home, your car, your golf clubs, your China collection, your RV, your Elvis memorabilia or any other toy or pacifier. You are *simply borrowing these things* for the short time that you are here on earth. You may think you own your stuff, but your stuff knows better. When you leave the planet, your stuff stays here—doesn't even wave good-bye—never sheds a tear! Your stuff knows that someone else will jump in and quickly take over your role as the *stuff collector* after you're gone. Someone else will live in *your* home, drive *your* car, swing *your* golf clubs, and dust off all that Elvis stuff. You won't be here but your stuff will. Heck, your stuff might even be around in the form of antiques at the turn of the next century. Talk about eternal life!

Let me come clean and admit that I too have a lot of stuff. Like most Americans, I love the feeling of purchase power—*never leave home without it*. Hey, my hobby is playing percussion—I have more hand drums, more tambourines, more shakers and cymbals, and cool little noisemakers than anybody I know. That reminds me; have you tried hand drumming as a way to combat stress? Oops! Sorry. Getting off on a tangent. I'll save that for another story…

What I have finally figured out—and hope you will too—is this: The good feelings that come from buying something new only last for a short time. That new car smell begins to stink as the monthly bills roll in. The big screen doesn't look all that big after a few months of watching it. All those clothes that you just had to have, will be out of date in a few short months. And here's the clincher—everything—absolutely everything—will eventually wear out, break down, rust, go out of style, get stolen, or just plain collect dust along with all your other stuff. But of course as soon as that happens, you'll be out buying more new stuff to replace all the old stuff—yikes! Do you see a pattern here?

Out with the old, in with the new—it's the American Dream and it's become an *addiction* for a lot of people. The code word used by those who are pushing the "more stuff drug" is *planned obsolescence*, and it's the way big business hangs on to you as a customer for life. Fortune 500 companies spend millions and millions of dollars every year trying to figure out how to get you to worship their *little tin god*—how to get you to buy more of their stuff after the stuff they already sold you wears out. They're good at it; it's how they stay in business and make their shareholders happy. But you don't have to play the game. You can stop the insanity, take charge of your purchase decisions and begin to make better life-choices regarding what will and won't make you happy.

How? By developing a strong sense of purpose and meaning in your life. Ever notice that when you are truly happy on the inside, you don't need much on the outside. Ever notice how many people try to compensate for an unhappy life by going out and buying something? The less that you need the more you will be able to *love the things that are truly important to you*. You will be able to say "NO!" to the unimportant stuff—the stuff that other people think you need—because there will be a stronger "Yes!" for the important stuff—the stuff *you know you need*—burning deep within you.

Who knows, you might even become a more peaceful and loving spirit. You might even become more concerned about giving stuff to other people than about getting more stuff for yourself. Maybe the stuff you begin to give away to others won't be stuff at all. Maybe it will be something much more important than stuff. Maybe it will be *love*.

The ability to give love—unconditional love—to others, comes from a peaceful soul—one that has surrendered, learned how to be still and is fully tuned into the power of spirit. As you begin to give more than you receive, receiving will begin to lose it's meaning for you. You will simply lose your interest for the *meaningless*—material possessions that have no meaning—and begin to focus on the *meaningful*—experiences and relationships that can truly make you happy. That's when the magic will begin to happen. That's when you will give up the need to worship a little tin god—the god that you buy with cash and credit cards—and begin to worship the real God—the God that lives in your heart and soul.

When you begin to see stuff for what it is—just stuff, you will never want to go back to your old way of life. You will continue to purchase things that you want—things that will support your *highest gift*—but you will do so with the knowledge that you really don't need these things to be happy. The power will come from *knowing you can have anything, but choosing to have only the highest things*—the things that line up with your individual truth; the things that support your purpose for living.

They buried my friend Bill at dusk, just as the California sun was calling it a day and laying its head down for a peaceful rest on the Pacific.

"He was a good man," the Pastor exclaimed.

He *was* a good man, I thought. A good man who now departs the world with the same possessions that accompanied his soul on the day he was born—he came with nothing and he leaves with nothing.

In the end, we will all leave with nothing. We will all clean out our closets, get rid of our stuff and take the final step towards love and light. We never know when that moment will come, we only know that it will. No amount of earthly possessions can prevent our final breath, our final heartbeat; our final departure from this *thing called life*. No amount of earthly possessions can substitute for experiencing true love, reaching out a helping hand to those less fortunate or helping to make the world a better place in the short time that we are here. But, I rest in the knowledge that in the end we will all return to the loving arms of spirit—naked, honest and pure. In the end, none of our stuff will matter. None of it matters now.

Some Things To Consider

How much emphasis do you place on your stuff? Do you own it or does it own you? Stop what you're doing right now and consider how many of your present moments—the only thing you really own—are being eaten up by the endless requirements of all your stuff. Is that how you want to spend your time on earth? If not, make plans now to sell or give away those things that no longer fit into your life's purpose. Eliminate the clutter in your life and watch your spirit rise to the occasion.

CHILDREN OF THE LIGHT

"It is written from the desert to the mountains they shall lead us.
By the hand and by the heart they will comfort you and me.
With their innocence and trusting they will teach us to be free..."

John Denver

Margaret stared off into the unfocused distance and tried to understand what had just been said. For the first time in her life she had received a clear understanding of what her purpose—her mission—was to be. There was no strike of lightening, no clap of thunder, just the unmistakable voice of God as He spoke to her heart. Tears of joy began to flow.

It had haunted her for the better part of her life, the little voice inside her head. She had heard it during moments when she was still enough to listen and honest enough to believe the words. Was she one of the chosen? One of the children born into the world to lead others—*by the hand and by the heart*—back to the place where they had come from?

Spiritual matters had always been on the forefront of her mind. Even as a little girl growing up on the back streets of Chicago, she had felt different somehow from all the other kids. Not alienated really, but definitely more aware of a higher being, a greater power. Her father had always called her "Margie the Saint," because of how she would always choose the path of love and kindness. Even the life of a small insect would be spared from the wrath of her fathers crushing shoe if Margie was around to intervene.

It had been a long journey this spirit trail, at times, difficult to navigate and often unfamiliar and unmapped. But throughout the past forty years, she just kept on believing that this day would come. That the light that

27

she was so aware of, would one day illuminate the world—even if it was her own small world, her own little corner of the planet.

She would work on her own doorstep first, she always thought. Start small and let God do the rest. If what she offered was needed on a larger scale, the world might beat a pathway to her doorstep. But that would be for God to decide. She would just keep *doing her part*. And there was plenty to be done.

For the past five years Margaret had written a column for the Chicago Tribune; a weekly piece on *spirituality in the workplace*. She had interviewed hundreds—if not thousands—of people who had stood up to be counted when their livelihood and their own careers were at stake. People who *chose the road of heart VS the road of convenience*. People with courage and strength. People who had made a difference in the lives of others. She named these enlightened souls and her column "Children Of The Light."

What began to amaze her, as time went on, was not so much that these types of people existed in every office throughout Chicago, but rather how they always seemed to show up in her life at just the right time and in just the right way. At first, she thought of it as mere coincidence, but the more it began to happen the more she began to believe that God was in fact pulling the strings. The heavens were responding and she was merely a passenger going along for the ride. Her fingers did the writing but it was quite clear that the words were not her own.

Then there were the God-like similarities between each of the people she interviewed. Not in a physical sense, but rather in the way they spoke, and smiled, and calmly but assuredly expressed their truth in a way that was non-threatening, open and honest. There was a glow about them as if they were being powered by an energy source unavailable to mortal man. They were just plain different and the differences were striking.

The thing that she always noticed first was the unconditional love and acceptance that they seemed to bestow upon everyone in their lives. There was never any jealousy, or unkind words. Never any haughtiness or pride. They just loved others the way they loved themselves. Giving the benefit of the doubt. Always rolling up their sleeves to help out when someone needed a kind and gentle hand.

While these people were seemingly powerful within their own circle of influence, their power was never based on anything they took away from another human being. Quite the opposite, really, their power seemed to be completely a bi-product of the power they freely gave away to others. So comfortable with themselves and their place in life, they were able to *get underneath the wings* of others and lift them up. By giving freely of themselves, they were rewarded with an abundance of love that flowed back into their lives in various forms. It was truly an amazing thing to witness.

She had exposed the presence of these so called "Children Of The Light" and fully understood that within the fabric of America and throughout the world, these individuals were quietly and without fanfare, going about the business of improving lives. Rather than complain about the darkness, each lit a single candle and allowed their light to provide direction and support to the vast majority of fellow human beings who appear all but blind to the wonder of God and His plan for their lives.

She too was one of them, and she knew it. A light worker. A messenger. A child of God. Her mission was just now becoming clear. But a mission it was and a mission it would be…

~ ~ ~ ~ ~ ~ ~ ~

"There should be less talk; a preaching point is not a meeting point. What do you do then? Take a broom and clean someone's house. That says enough."

Mother Teresa

She had seen enough false prophets to last a lifetime. They would phone her almost daily demanding that she interview them for her column. They were easy to spot, these self-righteous shysters. Boastful and arrogant, they would egotistically point to themselves and announce, "Come. I want you to see the wonderful things that I am doing." They looked good on the surface. But within their souls, in the places others could not see, they were living a lie. Their actions never lined up with their words. They were all talk and no walk.

But the so-called *Children Of The Light* were the real deal. There was a ring of truth in the way they lived their lives. There was nothing phony— no disconnect between their words and their actions. In fact, their actions were what set them apart from other well meaning and well intentioned souls who said all the right words but then never *did* anything.

Those who actually *walked in the light* lived their truth not with words but with actions, not with discussion but with demonstration. They knew that what they did was far more important than what they said. Rather than wasting time with clever conversation and verbal jousting, they simply rolled up their sleeves and went to work "sweeping the house of another." They knew their actions would *say enough.*

They would often describe themselves as "spiritual beings having an earthly experience" rather than the other way around. While some were Christians in the traditional sense, others were not. Many were Hindu or Taoist, while others were Buddhists, Jews, Islamic or New Age. Some had even developed their own truth based on their personal experiences with God and their individual walk along the spirit trail. Yet, there was a common thread that allowed them to accept the beliefs of others and *work side by side* in an environment of mutual trust and respect.

The word that best described it was *namaste—I will honor the place in you where we are all one.* It was this oneness that was so apparent, so noticeable. Each enlightened soul that she had interviewed had abandoned the need to force their beliefs on others and instead, surrendered to the common belief they all shared—a belief in a power greater than themselves. A belief in God.

By refusing to *draw lines in the sand*, they were able to come together and get things done as a collective force in their communities. Their spiritual beliefs were different. But, while they could have allowed those differences to alienate them, their *shared desire for a better world* became a more important issue—something they could rally around. Rather than differences, they focused on common ground. Rather than a "preaching point," they had found a "meeting point."

Margaret thought back to an interview she had done a couple years ago with a lady named Linda. Linda had spent the better part of her life believing that she, and those that believed as she did, knew the only way to God. She once remarked, "I was so wrapped up in this belief system that I began to look down my nose at anyone or any institution that didn't believe as I did. I never so much as listened to the opinions of others. I honestly thought that my way was the only way."

She went on, " My soul just opened up one day and I realized that my cold heartedness and self proclaimed *spiritual superiority* had resulted in nothing more than ten years of isolation. I had become a spiritual consumer, focused only on myself and my individual needs. I went to church to be entertained. It never dawned on me that God might expect a response from me in the form of action."

"Eventually, I saw that my self-righteousness was getting in the way of involving myself in life's only true pleasure—doing God's work. That's when I traded my so-called *superiority* for the opportunity to work with others—many who believe differently than I do—towards the collective goal of feeding the homeless. We opened a wayward shelter for those less fortunate to provide a place where homeless families can be fed in both body and spirit. I still believe what I believe, but now I *allow others the freedom* to do the same. This newfound freedom has allowed me to transcend religious boundaries and work with a diverse group of people in my community. Together, we are making a far greater contribution to the world, than any of us could have ever done alone."

Margaret began to consider, perhaps for the first time, that this collective spiritual energy—this coming together of diverse and different beliefs—was impacting the world in a powerful and positive way. Every good deed that was quietly being done—every small decency and justice that prevailed—each in its own way, eliminated the possibility that darkness could fill that space. More light, less darkness. Less darkness, more light. Could it really be that simple? Margaret's mind began to race with possibilities…

~~~~~~~~

"Someday, after we have mastered the winds, the waves, the tides and gravity, we shall harness for God the energies of love. Then for the second time in the history of the world, man will have discovered fire."

Pierre Teilhard de Chardin

In the days that remained of a life yet to be lived, Margaret would begin the journey home; a journey that would *begin with a spiritual awakening* and end with massive action. She bowed her head in prayer—to be still, to listen—to take in and absorb the power that would now illuminate her life as it had so many others. The voice of God—direct, comforting, honest— why had she fought these feelings for so long? Why had it been so difficult to surrender?

So many times before when life had chewed her up and spit her out, she had come to this resting place, on her knees, seeking mercy and grace. But this time it was different. This time, she vowed she would not rise to her feet only to return to her knees when the going got rough. No, this time, she would remain on her knees, perhaps for the rest of her life.

Up to this point, much of her time on earth had been focused on cheap entertainment. Something to numb the pain and distract her from the real work that she knew needed to be done. She had buried herself in her own little world, in acquiring material things and enjoying personal pleasures. She had climbed the ladder of success, but she could see now that it had been leaning on the wrong wall. The accomplishments that made her feel as if she were doing something noble, had only served to keep her sedated with pride and arrogance. She felt like a spoiled brat.

The nagging feeling in her heart, that she was headed down the wrong road, never went away, never retreated. But her life was comfortable and for anyone observing from the outside, perfect. Yet, on the inside, she was spiritually impoverished, *pacing the cage* and *starving for an authentic life.*

She had kept her own light hidden, afraid perhaps of what would happen if she simply let it shine. But now she had tapped into the power of God and for the first time began to experience a love that would allow her to do things she thought she could never do. It was time to reclaim her inner light and become her highest gift.

A few years ago, while conducting some research for an article she had written on the changing global community, she came across some very startling statistics. The numbers, based on what the world would look like if it were shrunk to a small village of precisely one hundred people, seemed to be tattooed on the inside of her forehead. She had tried to ignore them, but they would not go away...

- There would be 57 Asians, 21 Europeans, 14 from the Western Hemisphere and 8 Africans.
- 70 would be nonwhite while 30 would be white.
- 70 would be non-Christian, 30 Christian.
- A full fifty-percent of the world's wealth would be in the hands of only 6 people. All of these 6 people would be from the United States.
- 70 would be unable to read.
- 50 would suffer from malnutrition.
- 80 would live in substandard housing
- Only 1 would have a college degree.

It had become clear to her that somehow, we as Americans living in a world of abundance had *neglected the sanctity of human life*. We had become so focused on our own little piece of the planet that those less fortunate never hit our radar screen. *We had lulled ourselves into thinking that we could remain isolated forever*, oceans apart from the desperation and suffering we so often saw on the nightly news. We were monetarily wealthy and we believed our wealth would protect us.

But the *Children of the Light* had taught her a different lesson—that people operating from the heart could make a difference. From the elimination of racial hatred and the development of multicultural youth programs for the inner city, to a multinational task force focused on global peace building, to the development of spiritual tolerance that eliminates religious boundaries, a global movement of committed individuals could have an enormous impact on the future of the world. Like a laser beam, this collective spiritual power needs only to be focused with intensity and strength.

The solution was anything but practical. But then love is *never* practical. The solutions to our world problems cannot be addressed with the head. If we are to improve the state of the world, we must ask God to open the eyes of our heart. Only there will we find the ability to become humble and harness the energy of the spirit.

She thought for a moment of all the time and energy that had been wasted on matters of the head as opposed to matters of the heart. Why, for example do we have daily—even hourly reports—on the state of the war in Afghanistan but nothing is ever mentioned about the state of our children? Why is it OK to address our problems with hatred and violence but unacceptable or even a little wacko to suggest prayer and meditation as an alternative approach? Why do we entertain abortion research and intellectual dialog regarding the number of weeks after conception that physical life is born, without ever considering at what point, prior to conception, the soul is born?

Those and many other questions begged to be answered. The world was heading out of control, down the road of no return. Somehow, she had to do her part to change the course of history. She must take a stand and speak up for the light that lives within the soul of each of us. For we are all *Children of the Light*, each connected to the same invisible power of love. We can each make a difference. We need only believe it to make it so.

And so it would be, with the dawning of a new day, that the world would pause just long enough to be transformed. It would remember to treasure the virtues of love that are written within the soul and take a collective cleansing breath that would push away fear and allow the God Force to lift us up to a higher level of consciousness. The united energy of those individuals—those *Children of the Light*—brave enough to stand up and be counted, would indeed change the world forever.

Some Things To Consider

How are you letting your light shine in the world? List two things that you are currently doing to improve the world around you. List two more things that you could do if only you had a little help from your friends. Call your friends and see what can be done to get things moving.

Better Lives Begin with Better Choices

"Destiny is not a matter of chance, it is a matter of choice;
it is not a thing to be waited for, it is a thing to be achieved.

Unknown

When I hear others complaining about negative things happening in their lives, I am reminded that everything we have, everything we are, is a byproduct of the choices we make. Nothing happens to us that we do not choose, whether consciously or unconsciously. Want to have a better life? Make better choices.

Our health is a good example. When we complain that we feel tired, run down, overweight or stressed out, perhaps we need to realize it's because of the poor choices we've made. A sedentary lifestyle or one filled with too much fat, sugar, caffeine or alcohol, will not result in a healthy body. Dr. Bernie Siegel asks his patients, "Why did you *choose* this disease?" Optimum wellness is a choice!

And what about your career? Your mama didn't tell you to become a widget repairman! If you dislike your job and really want to make a contribution to society or express your true talents, heed the words of Nike and "Just do it!" The only thing standing in the way of the job or career you desire is you. Don't just sit around waiting for things to change to your liking because chances are they never will. You must be the change agent. You must manifest what it is you desire!

To make better choices and live the life of our dreams, we must focus on a couple of key questions. First, will this choice bring me closer to learning who I am and becoming who I want to be? We often make decisions and

choices too quickly without taking into consideration the long-term conse-
quences. Every decision today creates the world we will inherit tomorrow.
Or looked at another way—your life today is the sum total of all the
choices you made in the past.

Different choices take us down different roads. To make sure that the
road you choose will lead to your ultimate destination, it can help to
imagine it's your eightieth birthday. All of your friends and relatives have
gathered on this wonderful occasion to stand before you and describe all
of the magnificent accomplishments of your life. What will they say?
What would you like them to say?

After you have identified the accomplishments that will in essence
become your *legacy*, do what Stephen Covey says and "begin with the end
in mind." In other words, work backwards from where you want to end
up in your lifetime and make choices today that will lead you there. Don't
settle for anything less!

Next, I think it is important to determine on a scale of 1 to 10, whether
the choice you are about to make is your highest choice. How will you
know? Your highest choice will always be the one that is *void of any ego
attachment* and will reflect the inner direction of your soul. Normally,
your highest choice will not be the first choice that comes to mind because
the ego will usually override your soul and scream the loudest! The ego is
very clever and knows exactly how to distort what it is we really want.
Whenever I find I have made a poor choice, I usually realize that my ego
found a way to shut out my heart. It's as simple as that.

To quiet the ego and let your soul speak, you must be *out of your mind*.
In other words, you must turn your mind off and let your soul, heart and
feelings take over. Find some quiet time—get off by yourself— and without distraction, *learn to be still*. Then, move from the stillness to a meditative state. This will provide an environment in which the *voice of the soul*
can be heard. The soul, you see, is a rather polite fellow. It will always
remain quiet in the presence of more boisterous competition such as the

ego. Your challenge is to find a way to *get the ego to shut up* just long enough for the soul to speak.

During meditation, *try on* your various choices in the context of how you feel once you have made them. In other words, see yourself as having already made the decision. How does it feel? Do you feel lighter, happier, and full of energy? Or is there a queasy feeling in your gut? Repeat this exercise as many times as necessary until the decision lines up with your highest values and beliefs. Oh, and that little voice you're hearing in your head; listen to it! It's there to help you along the path.

Note: while we're on the subject of meditation, please understand that setting in the lotus position with your legs wrapped around your neck is not a requirement. Frankly, not many people can sit like that for any length of time. It may be a good way to learn to scratch your nose with your big toe but how often will that come in handy? Find a position that feels comfortable and relaxed so that you can focus your attention on shutting down the inner-chatter of your mind and finding the voice of your soul.

As we choose, so we become. Don't look back at your life from your eightieth birthday and wish things had turned out differently. Learn to make better choices today that allow you to leave the legacy you desire. Turn off the noise, turn up the silence and choose to become your highest gift. A better life awaits you!

Some Things To Consider

Do you accept full responsibility for the choices you make? Have the choices you've made in the past taken you to where you want to go? Pretend it's your eightieth birthday and all your friends and family have come to celebrate. Each will get up in front of the group and reflect on your many accomplishments. What will they say? What do you want them to say?

BICYCLES, BEER AND A WHOLE LOT OF WISDOM...

"Wisdom is the power that enables us to use knowledge for the benefit of ourselves and others."

Thomas J. Watson

"**L**ast one to the top buys the beer!" My friends and I had no idea who this guy was, but our competitive spirit took over as we mounted our bikes and began the treacherous climb to the top of Porcupine Rim.

It was extremely hot in Moab Utah—somewhere in the hundred-degree range—as I stood up on my pedals trying to get more torque. I had ridden Porcupine Rim before, but never in such extreme temperatures and certainly never at such a high rate of speed. It was about a one thousand foot ascent from where we were to the top of the rim. I was determined to get there first.

This guy is an animal, I thought, struggling to wipe the sweat from my face while keeping one hand on the handlebars. Moab claims ownership to some of the most difficult and challenging mountain bike terrain in the entire world. It has claimed the life of a few riders who pushed the envelope too far. That thought was never too far from my mind as I struggled to make it the last few feet before finally reaching the top.

"I'll take an ice cold bottle of Guinness," the unknown rider declared, as I humbly removed my feet from the toe clips and began to dismount.

" I can't believe you beat me. How long have you been waiting here?"

"Not long. Only about ten minutes. By the way, my name is Ben—Ben Stevens."

"Ten minutes! You must be a pro!"

"Well, I've been riding bikes since thirty-five. I guess I'm finally getting good at it."

"Since you were thirty-five? How old are you now?"

"No, I don't mean since I was thirty-five, but rather since 1935. As in nineteen hundred and thirty-five. I was actually born in 1929. You know, the end of the roaring twenties."

"A little warm today," Ben said, as he removed his helmet and sunglasses, to reveal a face much older than the fit and trim body that supported it.

"Hard to believe," he continued, "but if the good Lord is willing, I'll turn seventy next week. Some friends and I plan to celebrate while we do Ride the Rockies. Wouldn't miss that ride for all the tea in China."

We chatted for a bit before getting back on our bikes to ride the remaining five hours that would lead us through some very technical terrain. We rode together for a while; the time passing all too quickly, as this seventy-year-old mountain biker shared with me his philosophy on life. I listened intently as he explained how he had outlived three wives, all of his four brothers and sisters, both of his parents and God knows how many dogs and cats.

"You know, Ben, you remind me a lot of my friend Dick. He's about the same age as you and equally as fit. Dick runs his age about five or six times a week."

"Sounds like my kind of guy. But what do you mean, "runs his age?""

"He's sixty-seven, Ben. That means he'll run 6.7 miles a day this year and 6.8 miles a day next year and on and on. He runs almost everyday except Sunday."

"Now let me get this straight. Every year your friend's mileage increases as opposed to getting shorter. Hell, at that rate he'll be doing ten miles six times a week in another thirty years!"

We both laughed at the thought and then Ben said, "You know, I'm not joking. Your friend Dick will still be running at the age of 100 if he stays healthy and most importantly, believes he can do it. Most of the battle is in our minds."

"Yes sir, Dick sounds like one of those crazy people I hang out with," Ben continued. "Love to meet him some day."

As he spoke, I thought about my friends and myself. Most of us were half of Ben's age and many were already beginning to complain about the perils of getting old. Nothing worse than the whining of baby boomers approaching the half-century mark, I thought.

I completed Porcupine Rim in just under six hours. Ben had left me in the dust just after we hit the summit. Now, totally spent and dreaming of a hot shower, I threw my bike on the rack, climbed in my truck and stuck the key in the ignition. The endorphins were kicking in. All was well with the world!

My friends and I regrouped that evening at Eddie McStiff's, the local watering hole, to swap lies and down a few brewskies. Just as the attractive young lady was about to seat us, I glanced over at the bar and lo and behold, there was Ben holding court with a few of the locals.

"Forget the table. Let's eat in the bar. You guys have to meet someone."

A warm and friendly smile came across Ben's face as we sat our sore butts down and motioned for the bartender. "Hey old friend," Ben declared "Glad to see you made it back alive! Porcupine Rim—toughest ride I've ever done!"

After a few brief introductions, we ordered a couple pitchers of beer, several appetizers and one *ice-cold bottle of Guinness*.

"Guess I owe you this, Ben. Any chance we could continue the conversation we began earlier today?"

"Ahhh, an ice cold Guinness. Best damn beer in the entire world as far as I'm concerned. Nothing better—except perhaps mixing it with a little Bass Ale. Makes for a really fine Black and Tan. I like a man who keeps his word. Now what is it you'd like to talk about?"

"Well, Ben, there are a lot of things I would like to ask, but, frankly, I would love it if you would tell us your secret for remaining so youthful. I mean honestly, you seem much younger than you obviously are. In some ways you seem younger and more excited about life than many of us and we're half your age! How do we follow in your footsteps and keep the wrinkles away?"

"First off, forget the wrinkles," he said. "Getting old is 90% in your head. If you think or act old—you are old—no matter how many wrinkles you may have. It's as simple as that."

"OK, I agree with that. But beyond appearances what's the secret, Ben? I mean, how will we know when we are slipping off course—when getting old is getting the better of us?"

"Well, you must understand that getting old is a decision not a consequence," Ben continued. "Why, some folks are old at thirty while others seem to be getting younger every year well into their eighties and nineties. But there *are* a few things to watch out for. I mean, if these things begin to show up in your life, run like the dickens! Do an about face and make some changes quickly!"

Below are Ben's words of wisdom. Gratefully traded for one very cold bottle of Guinness Stout.

You will know your getting old when:

- You begin to down more Advil than all the M&M's you ever ate as a kid. Yoga and stretching exercises are the long-term solution. Forget the drugs. Stretch, stretch, stretch!

- You trade the fast lane for the fat lane. When you begin to trade the physical activity you enjoyed in your youth for a soft couch and a remote control, you're doomed. Never stop doing your sport, whatever it may be. Mind over mattress is the key.

- Gravity begins to affect your smile. It's true that over the years gravity wreaks havoc on our bodies. But it has nothing to do with your smile. Show the world your pearly whites! And by the way, I dare you to try to be in a bad mood while you're smiling. It's practically impossible.

- You exchange your passion for cynicism. Living is all about attitude. Attitude is all about having a passion for life. There is nothing worse than someone who is bah-humbug day after day—everyday. No one wants to be around people like that. Never lose you passion for living.

- You never venture too far from the comfort zone. Living a little on the edge keeps you fresh. Occasionally put yourself in a position to sink or swim. And for crying out loud, always continue to improve in every aspect of your life, including your hobbies. Always keep learning.

- You stop contributing to a better world, a better life. Do what you can with the life that you have been given. And don't forget to leave some unfinished business for tomorrow—it will help to get you out of bed the next day.

- You pay more attention to your hairline than your waistline. This one is more for the guys than the gals. Until they come out with a product that really grows hair, baldness is something men can't control. Your waistline, however, is within your grasp. Bald men don't look bad. But fat men, whether they have hair or not, look old. Stay fit and stay active.

- You begin to lose faith. Whenever I am feeling down or discouraged, I simply think about my Lord and Savior hanging on that cross. Nails through His hands and feet, the pain must have been excruciating. Compared to that, I can handle anything that might come along. I know this may not be politically correct—talking about Jesus and all— but I'm not running for office. It works for me. Pick the spiritual master that works for you and strive everyday to become more like them.

The bartender asked for last call as we raised a final glass to Ben. We thanked him for sharing his wisdom with us; paid the tab and headed back to the hotel for some much needed sleep. It had been a long and satisfying day.

As my head hit the pillow, I thanked God for having blessed my life with so many interesting friends and acquaintances. I am convinced that people come into our lives to either learn from us or teach us something. Ben taught me the meaning of living every day to it's fullest—no matter what age we are, no matter what obstacles have been placed in our way. Now if I could just find that bottle of Advil....

Some Things To Consider

Who has recently come into your life to learn from you? What did you teach them? Who has recently come into your life to teach you? What have you learned?

THE INFINITE POWER WITHIN

"We were all meant to shine as children do. We were born to manifest the glory of God that is within us. It's not just in some of us; it's in everyone. And as we let our own light shine, we unconsciously give other people permission to do the same."

Marianne Williamson

I grew up believing in the unlimited potential of all human beings—that each of us has the ability to harness the power of the God force within and manifest our own destiny. I never once doubted this infinite power of the Universe, a power that flows through each and every living thing with perfection and grace. I have always known that everyone is worthy to receive this power and draw upon it any time we choose.

The power I speak of is not limited, ego driven, special or available to only a few select individuals. It is abundant and available to everyone. This power has no bias, knows no boundaries and can be tapped into at any time. If you picture an oasis—a spring of life-giving water—a place where everyone of every race, color and creed can freely drink without fear, you will have come close to understanding this power.

If we let it, this power can direct our lives to a higher state of health, a higher state of love, a higher state of truth and a higher state of being. It will lead us through the darkness of the past and into the light of the future. It is as real as the sunlight yet as invisible as the wind. It can provide us with every answer to every question ever imagined, if only we would ask.

This power can provide us with all the wisdom and guidance we will ever need to navigate through this life. It can heal our wounds; both emotional and physical. It can lift our spirits and make us whole. There is nothing that cannot be accomplished the minute we become aware of this Universal energy. It runs through our very souls and is no further away than our hearts.

Sometimes we tend to over think it, intellectualize its presence, or attempt to reduce it to something that can be dissected and taken apart. But the minute we do so is the minute it will leave us, for it is perfect in its completeness ever constant yet ever changing. It is holistic in nature and the sum of all its parts. All spokes in the wheel lead to its center. All spiritual paths end at its doorstep.

We are not this power but it does live within us. It sets waiting, unbridled and focused, ready to come to life the minute we call upon its strength. We know it is there, deep within our souls, yet few of us ever use it. Instead, we let it lie dormant and untapped while ignoring its vast potential and allowing ourselves to settle for lives that are often less than the divine purpose we were meant to become.

Within its presence, the ego is all but demolished. For this power transcends all ego and *focus on self* and creates, instead, a loving environment where personal gain fits comfortably within the framework of group consciousness. No one loses when this power is brought into our daily decisions. No one loses because this power belongs to everyone.

This amazing power cannot be bottled or sold. It does not exclusively reside in a certain building, or a special book or within a particular group or religion. Its truth can be spoken by everyone—in different languages and with different interpretations—not just by those who choose to stand in front of others and proclaim its presence, but by every man, woman and child.

To access this power we need only to release ourselves from past patterns of behavior and allow our mind to subordinate itself to our heart. For this power lives within the heart and is manifested through our thoughts and our feelings. Through our thoughts it helps us to create our future. Through our feelings it allows us to understand our truth and become our highest gift.

Some are comfortable calling this power God; others are not. Some see this power as male, some female. Some see no sexual connotation whatsoever and instead envision a universal power that knows no gender. Some find this power in a church, synagogue or mosque while others find the same power while hiking through nature or within the imagination of their own minds. It makes no difference how we see it; only that we do. It makes no difference how we access it, only that we do. It makes no difference when or where we come to understand it; only that we do.

The power to control ones destiny lies in our ability to flow with this power and trust its infinite wisdom. We may hasten the journey by beginning to take responsibility for our lives and refusing—absolutely refusing—to blame others for our past mistakes. For there are no mistakes, there are only opportunities for learning. What we often see as failures are not failures at all, but simply another chance to understand what we are not. This understanding will move us closer to this Universal Power and bring us ever more clearly into its grace.

As I consider the awesomeness of this power, a power that I have come to trust, I am reminded of something I wrote several years ago. It's a short story about an aging grandfather and his ten-year-old grandson and brings forth an analogy of the very power I am speaking of. I would like to share a small piece of this story with you, so that perhaps you too will more fully understand the power within and begin to drink from this life-spring of Universal power and strength.

The young boy held the tiny seeds in his ten-year-old hand and began counting them one by one. "Twenty-four," he shouted to his grandfather, who gazed over at him from across the dusty field.

"Wonderful!" grandfather replied. "Twenty-four sunflowers. That should keep you busy this summer. It will be your job to tend the soil, remove the

weeds, do the watering and make sure they grow to be big and strong. Do you believe you can do it?"

"But there's nothing here, grandfather—they're just seeds," the young boy demanded.

"How will they ever turn into sunflowers? Heck, these seeds don't even look like sunflowers—there's no resemblance whatsoever. They just look like, well, seeds."

"Come," grandfather said. "I want to show you something."

Laying one of the seeds on a large stone, the wise old man quickly picked up another stone of equal size and upon slamming the two together, crushed the seed with a decisive blow that turned it into nothing but powder.

"Look," he said. "Do you see anything moving?"

"No," the grandson replied.

"Look again!" the grandfather demanded. "Look again!"

"Nothing. Grandfather. I don't see a thing!"

"That's the point, son," the grandfather replied. "The power of the universe is invisible and because we cannot see it we think it does not exist. Yet in truth, we do see it everyday of our lives. For everything in this life is of its power. We have simply forgotten that it is so."

"You see," he continued, " if we trusted only our physical senses it would seem that there is nothing within this seed that will amount to much. But if we were to look closer, with a very powerful microscope, we would see the energy of life—God's energy—vibrating within the seed just as it vibrates in everything. The power is within the seed even though we can't see it. Why, it's the same energy that your mother and father used to create you. The same energy that runs through you today."

"But I'm not a sunflower, grandpa," the little boy laughed.

"No, son, you're not a sunflower. But you are connected to the same Source—the same life force that flows through every living thing on this planet and beyond. There is nothing here that was not perfectly created—you included. God's power and energy lives in us all. The same energy that will transform this seed into a beautiful sunflower, will transform you from a child to a man and allow you to become anything your heart desires."

"But, wait a minute, grandfather. "Even if we plant the seeds, water them, and tend the soil, how do we know they will grow?"

"It's at that point that we must take a leap of faith, son," grandpa replied with a serious grin.

"Not blind faith mind you," he continued, "but faith based on the power that God has bestowed upon us, the universal power that lives within. We must have faith that this life force is without bias, nonjudgmental and abundantly flows through everything and everyone—including sunflower seeds—in equal amounts and with the same results—life! Even though we can't see it, we know that it exists, for time and time again it has manifested itself in a newborn baby, a drop of rain, the petals of a flower, a litter of kittens. We must have faith and believe in this power. Our belief will make it so."

"Our belief will make it so." I would even go one step further and suggest that our thoughts, the ideas that make up our beliefs, will make it so—or not so—depending on what we think about. The Universe will respond to our thoughts and bring them to life. As my mother use to say, "Be careful what you wish for."

The God force within each of us mandates that *what we think about expands* and becomes our reality. Our thoughts create our truth and ultimately our experience of this thing called life. Want to change your life? Change your thoughts—it really is that simple. But many of us are unwilling to embrace this truth. Instead we hand over the power to define and shape our own lives to others. We don't trust the Universe and our place in it and consequently, we don't trust ourselves to make Divine choices. We want someone else to make the decisions for us.

But by not choosing we are in effect *choosing not to choose*. The result is that we settle for whatever life hands us—often not the things we desire—because we believe that we are not in control. The fact is, that while our egos are not in control, the God force is. And because the God force resides in us, we are very much in control. Our power lies in our ability to reduce the endless desires of the ego and let our Godliness prevail. By doing so, we can co-create with God the life we desire.

Dr. Wayne Dyer, a spiritual master whose teachings I have studied for some twenty-five years, sums it up like this: "Destiny is not preordained. Destiny is ordained totally by you. Every single moment of your NOW existence is the result of your previous thought. The idea that everything is already laid out for you in advance is a hallucination. You can and do manifest your own destiny."

We are all equally important in the eyes of the Universe. Each of us has a Divine Purpose—that which we were born to do. But to achieve our life's purpose, to become who we were meant to be, we must first tap into our God-given power and allow the Universe to bring into our lives the desires of our hearts and the true manifestation of our authentic selves.

You see, over the centuries, God has heard our prayers for a better world and He continues to send us help 24/7, within the potential of every newborn child. It may be hard to believe sometimes with all of our self-imposed roadblocks and negative self-talk, but we—you and me—are the only hope for a better tomorrow. God gave each of us His power and He's just waiting for us to use it. Don't play small. Don't fear your own Divine potential. Plug into the power within and let your light illuminate the world!

Some Things To Consider

If you could do anything, what would it be? Why aren't you doing it? Think about all the masters that walked the earth—Jesus, Buddha and all the others. Take a look at all the miraculous things they did with their lives. They represent the potential in all of us. We may never reach their level of enlightenment but we must try. See if you can move just one step closer to becoming more like them. See if you can move one step closer to living your dreams.

RELATIONSHIPS

Relationships…. We all want 'em. We all got 'em.
What are we gonna do with 'em…?

Jimmy Buffet

"**I** need someone to complete me," Susan said. "Someone who will make me whole. Someone who will provide the other half of who I was meant to be. My soul mate must be out there somewhere…"

Susan had spent the better part of a lifetime searching for a soul mate. Three marriages and as many painful divorces later, she was still desperately looking for Mr. Right—a man who would be *her knight in shining armor.*

I'd heard it all before of course—how two rather incomplete people could come together and become one. But, I never really bought into the notion of two emotional invalids making each other whole. After all, didn't God make us in His own image? Aren't we already complete? Already (w)holy?

Through movies, books and music, we have come to believe that to be truly happy we must connect somehow and fall in love—romantic love—with another human being. We are brainwashed to believe that true happiness lies *outside ourselves* in the arms of that "special person". Of course relationships are important, but only if we are willing to truly be ourselves and focus more on what *we can give to another* rather than on what we can get. By focusing on giving to others through our own unique gifts and talents, we will attract others into our lives with abundance.

51

To attract others, we must be the real deal. No compromising here. We must become our true selves and then project our truth into the world around us. By telling the world "This is who I am" the universe is free to respond accordingly as the people, places and things around us begin to assist us in the manifestation of our destiny. By giving to others the gifts that make up our true selves, we say to the universe "This is what I truly have to offer. How can these gifts be of help?"

By fully engaging in who we truly are, we no longer need to search for friends, lovers or so-called "soul mates." We begin to understand that searching for another human being to complete us is a losing proposition because no one on earth holds the missing pieces that will make us whole. We need only to look within ourselves, to the God Force within, for it is there that our completion lies. Our relationship with Him is what will make us (w)holy.

My friend Jim just met the woman of his "dreams". He explained to me one night how he had been on his best behavior when he was around her. "I don't want to blow this one," he said. "I need a relationship."

"Not if you aren't being honest about who you are," I replied. "You need to be yourself, Jim—warts and all."

"But she could be my soul mate," Jim continued. "The one I have been looking for my entire life. I can't risk losing her."

"If she is your soul mate, you can be sure she will want to know the real you," I offered. "After all, the soul harbors the truth. If your soul is to "mate" with another, it can only do so when the relationship is based on trust—the end result of expressing your truth. The two of you may become one, but *who will be the one the two of you become* if you're not being honest about who you are? Do you really want to give up that much of your truth just to have a relationship?"

True relationships are based on support and healing. They are never about what we can get from another, but, rather, what we can give. But for the healing to take place, for powerful relationships to be born, we must first show each other our scars. We must bear our souls and truly express who we are. We can't "fake it" and wear only a happy face. By sharing our pain with each other, we "come clean" with ourselves and encourage love to seek an entrance through our open wounds.

When we develop relationships based on a mutual sharing of our life stories, our pains, our wounds, we begin to detoxify our souls. We allow our friends, our lovers, to assist in the healing as we do the same for them. We expose our true selves knowing full-well that others may not find us appealing. But we also know that we would rather be rejected for being who we are, than be accepted for being something or someone we are not. The power comes from being ourselves and letting others decide if they want to be part of our lives. In bare-bones terms, we must scream at the top of our lungs "Take me for who I am or don't take me at all!"

And then there's the need for perfection. Many of us want only "perfect" relationships. You know, the hassle-free kind where the other person behaves exactly the way we want them to; sterile, low maintenance friends who don't require a great deal of "baby sitting". We want to *stay within our comfort zones* and not have to listen to other people's problems. "Just show me your good side," we say. "Take your problems to a shrink."

But guess what? You will never grow or learn the lessons you came to earth to learn by hanging around people who never challenge you. If someone knows *how to push your buttons* and bring out the worst in you, thank them! They are showing you the areas in your life where your ego is still in charge. That's probably why you chose to bring them into your life in the first place.

If we really want to grow from our relationships, we must allow others to freely express themselves. We must take it all in and *learn from their mistakes* without allowing our own inner-peace to be compromised. We must surrender our own agenda and allow the relationship to synergistically unfold. We must learn to love unconditionally. We must learn acceptance and become more God-like. Let's face it; this is tough stuff!

God wants us to engage in relationships that teach us how to love more purely. He wants us to learn how to relate to others the way He relates to us—with unconditional love. To learn this lesson, we must love others *for who and what they are*, not who or what we want them to be. The moment we can do this, is the moment we know that our relationship with another human being is *genuine and honest*. We must be willing to say "I accept you just as you are."

Of course, not everyone will befriend us. But just as a miner pans for gold, the relationships that were *not meant to be* will fall through the sifter exposing the wonderful friends, lovers and acquaintances that will enrich our lives and more clearly define our path. These (w)holy relationships will be based on truth and honesty. They will serve to reveal us for who we really are.

Just as relationships can add life and vigor to our earthly experiences, so too can they be *toxic*. In fact, continuing the relationship with the wrong person can be *down right fatal*. Physical abuse is an obvious life threatening bi-product of a bad relationship, but verbal abuse and the need for control can be just as damaging. I have often contemplated why some seemingly "normal" individuals stay in relationships of abuse. Then I met Carol...

We met over the telephone after she had read one of my columns and called to say how much *the main character reminded her of herself*. I do a great deal of writing and it took me a minute to remember exactly which story and character she was referring to. And then it suddenly struck me! She was comparing herself to a character that had endured a *lifetime of verbal abuse* under the hurtful words of an abusive and alcoholic husband.

As she told me her story, we both cried until a sudden silence fell over our conversation. "I can't just give up on him you know," she finally whispered. "It's the only thing close to a relationship I have ever had. I believe God has kept me here for a reason. But, now, leaving seems like the best thing to do. It will be painful but I need to do whatever it takes to help him."

"Perhaps giving up and getting out is exactly what you need to do Carol," I responded. "Actions speak louder than words. By leaving him, you may be *teaching him the lesson* God had in mind all along."

Carol's experience demonstrates that in many cases our relationships with others are *assignments from the God Force*; assignments that we must all take seriously. People come into our lives for one of two reasons: *To teach us or to learn from us*. Nothing is accidental when it comes to our involvement with other human beings. We enter into each other's lives for the divine purpose of enlightenment *and better understanding of our own truth*. It all sounds so wonderful but often the journey is anything but. Especially when we're doing the teaching.

The relationships that feel the most draining, as if we are not getting anything out of them, are often the ones where we're called to do the teaching. In Carol's case, she finally separated from her abusive husband, and in doing so, taught him a very important lesson about how to treat another human being. He is currently in counseling surrounded by other loving individuals who have been "assigned" to him. She walked away. He woke up. Had Carol not had the strength to play the *teaching role*, her husband (who she recently returned to), may have never *changed*.

In the end, it seems that improving our relationships is *more about changing our hearts and minds* than about changing our partners or friends. By refocusing on our spiritual walk and our oneness with the divine universe, by projecting our true selves into the world, we will uncover the person we were meant to be and help others to do the same. We will begin to attract into our lives those souls that God has assigned to us and push away the toxic relationships that serve no useful purpose. We will see that we are complete just as we are, for we were created in the image of God, our loving and eternal *soul mate*.

Some Things To Consider

Effective immediately: Let love flow from your life and into the world. Change your mind about how you see others and embrace them with kindness. Let your heart hang a little further down your sleeve and let people see your scars and the authentic you. The energy you send out into the world is what will come back to you in the form of relationships. Send out genuine love, with honesty and grace, and that is precisely what will return.

YOUR LAST FIVE MINUTES

*"There's got to be more to life than sittin' here watchin'
Days of Our Lives and foldin' your Fruit Of The Looms."*
Mama—Mama's Family

"Paging Mr. Hall, Mr. Jeffrey Hall. This is God's assistant calling. Our records show that you have only five minutes left to live. Please finish up whatever it is you *meant to do* while you were alive—the things that you thought you would get to *someday* but never did. Take one last look around and tell the people you care for just how much you really love them—all the things you *wanted to say* but didn't. Prepare to depart. The meter on your *earthly parking space* is about to expire." Say WHAT!!!

At some point in our lives, each of us will have just five minutes to live. Our last breath of crisp clean air, the last magnificent sunrise, the last person we touch; the last time we get to make any meaningful contribution to the world may be tomorrow—tonight—this very moment. None of us knows the precise time we will die; but we all know we will. It's a proven fact. In the physical sense, *nobody gets out of here alive.*

So why is it a lot of us (and you know who you are), live as if we might be the exception? We make other plans, put off important decisions, keep our true feelings to ourselves or temp fate as if we might be able to pull off what the great Houdini could not. Which reminds me, how did he do that underwater escape stuff anyway? I'm thinking mirrors, lots of mirrors...

Now hear me loud and clear: **People have been leaving our planet in record numbers for a long, long time.** It's true folks! I've done my homework here and it seems that there is a very clear and obvious trend that begins to occur *somewhere around the beginning of mankind* right up until the present moment—people die—lot's of people—all the time! *Death is claiming more lives everyday than all diseases put together!* Did I say that right?

I'm not making this stuff up! I used a lot of *scientific formulas and calculations*—this is a very real epidemic. For example, just about everyone born before 1850, with possible exception of a woman in Toledo named Zelda, are dead. They all checked out during the past 200 years. No one has heard from them since—no one! (By the way, word has it that Zelda hangs out at a health food store and lives exclusively on yogurt and brown rice. You can expect her new diet book to come out this fall.)

The other interesting thing I've noticed is that all kinds and types of people die. Its not like a lot of things here on earth where the rich or the incredibly good looking have a leg up. No, no, my dear friends, this appears to be happening to everyone regardless of wealth, sex, race, gender or creed. You may live a few years longer if you take good care of yourself— can you say *exercise*? But, *net-net*, bottom line—we get old—we wither up—we die. Makes those late night wrinkle cream infomercials seem a little silly doesn't it? Although I still like that Thighmaster thing…

The other day my baby-boomer friend Margaret remarked how *concerned she was* with the seemingly vast numbers of people in her life who were either dying or were deathly ill. "It's a *weird* feeling," she said. "I never thought people my age would just get old and die like everyone else. I've always thought of myself as young."

"But lately," she continued, "when I look in the mirror I see more and more of my mother's face every day. Do you know what I mean?"

Well, not exactly, I thought. I mean, I looked in the mirror the other day, but damned if I could see her mother's face. I did, however, see the face of some middle aged, balding guy with more new hair growing in his ears than on his head. This guy—who looked a whole lot like my father—scared the hell out of me! Who was that dude?

My purpose here is not to bring everybody down with a thousand words of the obvious. But, rather, I hope to put a subtle foot—or perhaps a not-so-subtle foot—*up the butts* of those of us who think we can continue to waste time and put off until tomorrow what we know we should be doing with our lives, today. You know, the important things—the things that really matter? The things that gnaw inside of you and keep you awake at night. No, I'm not talking about that fourth slice of pizza you inhaled at 11:00pm. I'm talking about your future, your destiny, your legacy—your life! Hellooooo!!!

Are we tuned into the same channel here? Can you hear me—over? I'm talking of the things you've always wanted to try? The things or thing you always knew you could be? Or maybe it's something special and loving that you've always wanted to say to another human being but were *just plain afraid* to let it out. My uncle Fred always wanted to tell my aunt Stella how much he adored that little black mustache that developed over her upper lip. It was kind of like one of those "Got Milk?" commercials, only for the *chocolate* variety. She sort of looked a little bit like Groucho Marx. Used to scare us kids half to death! Strange guy my uncle Fred…

It's nothing to be ashamed of, you know. Everybody has them; dreams, I mean. You know; your deepest desires—the things, that if you only had five minutes to live, you would want to run right out and do them. Some of us will connect with our dreams and live our bliss, while others of us will take them to the grave. *Grave.* I'm talking 6 feet under—Gonesville— DEAD! I looked up "dead" in the dictionary. It means **DEAD**!

I've come to believe that every song unsung—every life half lived— in some way, shape or form, damages all of mankind. Every potter who gives up the wheel because the world demanded a more *responsible* career; Every poet who timidly keeps her words to herself because way back in high school someone made fun of her; Every dancer who hides the rhythm in his feet because his college buddies might think he's something less than *macho*; Every women who gives up on being a mom because she thinks

time has passed her by and on and on, on and on. The clock is ticking—
tic-tock, tic-tock. Do I have your attention yet??

Do me a favor, OK? Sometime today—don't put it off until tomorrow—
get quiet and still. Kick the dog out of the bathroom if you have to, but find
a quiet place where you can just sit and think for an hour or so. Soak in the
tub, relax in the garden, get away from the kids if you have them and find a
little peace of heaven where you can just *shut down* and relax.

Now, close your eyes and try to pretend it's your eightieth birthday. A
party has been held in your honor. Present, are all of your closest friends, family and acquaintances. Hey, you can even pretend they still have their teeth!

Everyone has been asked to stand up before the group and speak of
your specific accomplishments and how you have personally impacted
their lives and the lives of others. What will each person say? What would
you like for them to say? Will you be proud of what you've done with your
eighty-years or disappointed in yourself?

Pretty heady stuff, eh? But, when you really stop and think about it, our
legacy is really *the only thing we can leave behind.* It's the footprint that
says, "I was here" long after we are not. Building a legacy is no small task.
It begins by *living our purpose* and making the most of every minute of
every day. Stephen Covey likes to say, "Begin with the end in mind." I
think that's a good way to look at it. Begin with where you want to end up
in life and then work backwards; making choices that will take you to the
destination you desire.

You see, just as there was a beginning to our physical life, there is also
an end to our earthly existence, when our souls will be reborn into a new
life in another dimension. Whether your day to depart the planet is five
minutes or five decades from now really doesn't matter. What does matter,
is that you recognize that your time here on earth is very limited and in
relationship to eternity, is about as short as the gap between two words in
a paragraph—dash, comma, period—the end!

Whatever it is you plan to do during your brief visit here, do it now.
Turn up a little Bonnie Rait and let her words really sink in, "Time gets

mighty precious when there's less of it to waste." Yes Bonnie, it does. Life's parking meter is indeed running and eventually we will all be out of time. Hey! Anybody got an extra quarter?

Some Things To Consider

Pretend for a moment that you have only five minutes to live. What is the first thing that pops into your mind? Focus on only that thing and understand that whatever it is, it is the key to discovering how every minute of your time here on earth should be spent. Now, what do you plan to do about it?

Perfect Balance

"Balance is a dynamic state of being,
a place where our mind and body and spirit can converse in concert, move
with subtle grace and behold its perfect intention."

Dr. James Rouse

There I was, five years old and sixty wobbly feet away from what seemed like the gazillionth "You can do it!" gentle push of my fathers guiding hands. When suddenly, for no apparent reason, I started losing my balance and soon found myself flying over the handlebars of a new—and without training wheels—Schwinn two-wheeler. Scraping across our driveway, head-over-tea-kettle (what exactly does that mean?) and at warp speed, the soft skin on my kneecaps and elbows soon parted company with the rest of my body and painfully took up residence somewhere on the rough concrete below. Can you say "OWIE!"

I finally came to an abrupt halt with the bicycle painfully wrapped around my body and my head stuck to the base of an old oak tree. Within seconds, a crowd of concerned onlookers (OK. It wasn't actually a crowd but more like four or five people and an old Labrador retriever) had gathered, including my mother who was screaming something about "putting my eye out!" and "cracking my head open!" (By the way, did you ever know anyone who actually "put their eye out" or "cracked their head open?")

Mom held me in her arms and proceeded to do the mommy thing, which meant asking if "I was alright" while at the same time telling me that I would "never ride that damn bike again!" Dad, who was usually the calm one, took decisive action and raced into the house, apparently looking for the first aid kit. Note: Recently, it has been determined, that at that precise moment the Detroit Tigers were on T.V. with the bases loaded and Kaline at bat. So it's a little fuzzy as to whether or not dad actually returned with the first aid kit or someone had to go find him…

Me? I was laughing my butt off and, well, shall we say, thrilled! Finally, after weeks of trying, falling down and trying again, I had found my balance and actually rode my bike—all by myself—to the end of the driveway with all of my friends looking on! Balance? I suddenly knew what it felt like, and at that moment, I was the only kid in the neighborhood (under the age of six) that did. Plus, I was wounded, bleeding and somewhat of a legend in my own mind. Evil Kenevil look out!

Remember when you first learned to ride a bike? Remember the difficulty of trying to balance on two thin tires? It was hard, but you were eager to learn. You kept at it. You never gave up. Then suddenly, without really trying, the balancing part just sort of showed up. There you were, preparing to fall down once again, or, as my mom would say, "crack your head open" when all of a sudden the balance gods smiled on you and the next thing you know, you're riding high in the saddle! It was still the same old you, still the same old bike. The difference? You had found your balance. Life would never be the same.

Just as with riding a bike, perfect balance is essential to living a happy and healthy life. The struggles we face in our daily lives can seem just as overwhelming as learning to ride a bike did; until that magic moment when we achieve perfect balance. Yes, occasionally we may fall down, get frustrated or even desire to take the easy way out and return to our old habits. But eventually, as we continue to push on toward our dreams, respect our minds and bodies and tune into Spirit, the universe will allow perfect balance to show up in our lives.

My friend and fellow life coach Dr. James Rouse believes as I do, that true balance must involve body, mind and spirit. It is in balancing these three elements that we are able to discover our true path in life and manifest our destiny. By achieving perfect balance, we will reduce the stress in our lives and arrive at a sense of well-being; of knowing we are on-purpose and becoming our highest gift. We will find peace within ourselves and experience a sense of bliss not unlike that referred to as "Heaven on earth."

According to medical research, stress is the cause of 98% of all disease! Folks, we're not only talking about heart attacks, strokes or immune system breakdowns here, but, with the exception of two viruses, every single disease known to man. Plain and simple: stress kills! There is a definite correlation between the elimination of stress and the creation of optimum health and perfect balance. As balance and improved health increase, stress and disease decrease. The opposite is also true—as stress increases, our ability to find balance diminishes and our health declines.

The good news is that science and spirituality are beginning to come together as a powerful force. Hundreds of research studies clearly document the link between body mind and spirit, and for the first time, medical doctors are attending conferences on faith and healing in record numbers. As baby boomers are watching their parents get older, and witnessing the same effects of aging in themselves, alternative forms of medicine focused more on prevention than treatment are becoming commonplace in our society. The conclusion: Perfect balance of body, mind and Spirit can prevent, and in some cases, heal a multitude of health problems.

In my own life, I have found the connection between body, mind and Spirit to be a tremendous source of strength. When all three are equally balanced and as coach James says, "conversing in concert" I am at my best. I do my best work and give genuine love and attention to myself and those around me. I feel good about who I am, don't kick the dog so much and simply put: I am a better human being all the way around.

But, when one of these three areas are out of balance, so is my life. I miss deadlines, eat the wrong foods, get angry, lose my cool and create misery for those around me. When I am out of balance, just as when I fell off my bike, life becomes a struggle—I am out of control.

What follows is a brief review of body, mind and Spirit. No rocket science here—just simple tried and true ideas that have created balance and optimum health in my life and in the lives of many others. Will they work for you? Absolutely! Give them a try (after consulting your physician) and let me know what you think. As we walk this Spirit trail together, my prayer is that you too will find balance in your life and become your highest gift.

Body. Our bodies support our souls as we navigate the planet. Keeping our bodies healthy is tantamount to insuring that we are as productive as possible during the short time that we are here. It's not so much about quantity or how long we will live, but rather about quality or how well we will live.

The body houses our mind and soul and depending on how well we take care of it, will allow us or prevent us from playing an active role in our own universe. If we are over weight, suffering from poor nutrition, or otherwise physically run down and out of shape, our lives and the lives of those around us will suffer. It is difficult to traverse the Spirit trail; to ascend to the highest levels of being, if we don't like our bodies or have the energy it takes to get out of bed in the morning! Mind over mattress requires optimum energy and optimum energy can only come from a body that is finely tuned.

A sound body requires proper nutrition and proper nutrition means getting the proper amount of vitamins and minerals everyday of our lives. That means taking supplements. Often our schedules don't allow us to eat the right combination of foods necessary for optimum health. To achieve your desired level of fitness, at minimum, a good pharmaceutical-grade multi-vitamin combined with additional doses of pharmaceutical-grade vitamin C and E should be taken everyday. Your vitamin and mineral regime can be much more involved than this, but this is a good place to start if you are considering nutritional supplementation. Consult with a knowledgeable nutritionist for further information and options.

We've all heard it said for years, and it's true: It makes good sense to reduce the excess fat in your diet, particularly animal fat. Don't feel like you have to cut out everything you've been eating for the past forty years overnight. Just reduce your intake of red meat, butter, cheese and other dairy products gradually over time. Eat more chicken and fish, try a small amount of jam without butter on your toast, and have your burger without cheese for a change. If you feel like living a little on the edge, try replacing cow milk (or as I like to think of it, "the bodily fluid from an animal") with soymilk. Look for a product called Silk in your grocer's dairy case—it's awesome! Also, think about replacing the typical three square meals with six smaller meals spread out across the day. This will help to keep you mentally balanced by keeping your blood sugar level in check.

Next, consider eliminating or at least reducing your consumption of alcohol, sugar and caffeine. Studies have shown that people who abuse alcohol also drink a significant amount of caffeine every day. Here's the connection: caffeine consumption results in a sharp drop in blood sugar levels. Alcohol on the other hand, is one of the most concentrated forms of sugar known to man. Thus, after a long day of too many latte's and cappuccino's, your body will be searching for a way to replace the lost sugar. Alcohol fits the bill perfectly. It's a vicious and unhealthy cycle of too much caffeine during the day followed by too much alcohol at night.

Note: It has been said that moderate alcohol consumption is OK. That's because alcohol, like other potentially toxic substances, is essentially a poison. Moderately poisoning yourself is indeed better than completely poisoning yourself! But, why poison yourself at all? Eliminate this junk from your body and get off the caffeine/alcohol roller coaster. Spiritually speaking, you don't need any external substance to alter your state of consciousness—the power to feel good is within you! Replace alcohol and caffeine consumption with purified or spring water—drink at least half your body weight in ounces every day. Weigh 150lbs? Drink at least 75 ounces of water daily. Simple.

When it comes to exercise, there are three areas that most fitness experts agree must be incorporated into any daily work out program: aerobics, stretching, and weight training. My own personal exercise program consists of yoga and meditation at sunrise, followed by twenty minutes of weight training, followed by a forty-five minute run. A couple of good books to get you headed in the right direction are, Body for Life by Bill Phillips and Yoga for Dummies by Georg Feurstein and Larry Payne. Note: You don't have to be a pretzel to enjoy the benefits of yoga. Take a class to get acquainted with the concepts and poses. If nothing else, focus only on the breathing techniques. Learning to breathe properly will eliminate a significant amount of stress from your life. Yoga dates back 5000 years and currently some fifteen million Americans include some form of yoga in their fitness regimen—twice as many as did five years ago! This stuff works. Honest!

Try to get at least 8 hours of sleep each night. It has been estimated that most Americans fall at least an hour short of the eight-hour minimum and frankly some people need more than eight. Consider sleep to be a sacred requirement of each day. Let your body, mind and Spirit rejuvenate and rebuild themselves during your eight hours of living in dreamland.

Mind. The mind is truly a "terrible thing to waste" yet that is precisely what many of us do. We read too few books if any at all, watch far too much T.V. and consume mind altering substances that prevent us from honestly experiencing the joys of life. Feed your mind junk food and the result will be a junk-filled mind. Clarity of purpose and focused thinking are the result of a clear and focused mind. Remember: Everything we experience in life begins as a thought. As we think so we become.

Essentially, life is meaningless. Except for the meaning that we choose to give it, life has no agenda of its own. To give life meaning, you must be awake, involved and actively participating in the daily choices and opportunities that present themselves. Look at life like a blank slate; an empty canvass just waiting for the artist (that's you!) to determine what the painting will look like. How would you like to design your life? What would you like your legacy to be? What will your friends and family say about you after you are gone? Take the time to think about such things; don't let life simply happen to you. You truly do have the God-given power to create the world you choose to live in and manifest your desired destiny. The choice to do so is entirely up to you.

Connect with friends and family. Your family may consist of a spouse and children, a spouse and no children, children and no spouse, your mother, father and six hundred relatives or simply you and your dog. Whatever your family and circle of friends look like, take the time to listen to and deeply understand the people in your life who really matter. Let your heart hang a little further down your sleeve and openly express the love you feel for others as if you had only one more day to live. Who knows; maybe one more day is all you will get. Someone's last day on earth is today. Another group of us will be leaving the planet tomorrow. Let your family and friends know how much they mean to you—now!

A Course In Miracles states that "nothing occurs outside our minds." Meditation, prayer, tai chi and yoga can provide our minds with a silent sanctuary in a world that has become far too noisy. While there are many techniques for learning how to meditate—and I would certainly recommend buying a good book—for beginners it doesn't have to be that complicated. The whole idea is learning to be still—something we Americans have a tough time doing.

Try this: get up early in the morning—just before sunrise—and simply allow your mind to free float. Begin by giving thanks and gratitude to the Creator for all the blessings that have been bestowed upon you and your family. You will be surprised at how many good things happen to you on a daily basis when you really stop and take time to consider them. An attitude of gratitude can change your entire outlook on life.

Think of meditation as mental floss and just let your mind relax as the cobwebs from a good night's sleep begin to dissipate. Replace any and all negative thoughts that creep into your psyche with positive affirmations as you anticipate the start of a new day. What good things do you want to happen in your life and in the lives of others? Repeat those things to yourself. As you do this and without any straining, breathe in deeply from your stomach and exhale each breath as slowly as possible. Visualize your life as you want it to be. Go within yourself to find all the answers you need for the challenges the new day will surely bring. Try this for several mornings and then tell me how much better you feel! Remember: When you're not going within you're going without!

Spirit. The Spirit Trail will be different for each of us. There is no one-way to connect with God, there is only your way to connect with God. Like spokes on a wheel, there are many different ways to reach the center and connect with the Creator. Don't feel guilty if your way is not the same as someone else. That's why there are so many different options; so many different churches, synagogues, mosques, temples, religions, denominations, faiths, beliefs, perspectives, groups, and individual truths about the God Force. God lives in all of us and is therefore uniquely accessible to every human being in a language that will be as individual and as diverse as we are. Find the language that works for you, take a leap of faith and most importantly, believe!

Let your belief manifest itself into action—live your truth authentically and with passion so that others will see you as a light worker and holy example. There is nothing worse than professing to believe something but behaving in ways that don't line up with what you believe. I have personally witnessed, as many of us have, television evangelists, pastors of major churches, spiritual writers and speakers and so-called men of faith, who speak so righteously in public but live their lives like heathens when they think no one is looking! Don't let this happen to you Live what you believe and allow others to do the same.

Learn to meditate and pray alone. Get comfortable with the silence and simply listen. God doesn't just speak to some people; He speaks to everyone. You don't need anyone or anything to act as an intermediary between you and God—He doesn't need a translator, He just needs your attention. Look at it this way: You came into this world alone and you will leave this world alone. Eventually, each of our souls will leave the planet and commune with God one on one. Why not start now?

Even though I have listed Spirit as the last concept in the body, mind and spirit triad, it is, in actuality, the first area we should focus on as we seek balance and optimum health. It is common to think that we must get ourselves together—perfect our body and minds—before we connect to Spirit. In fact, it seems that just the opposite is true; once we surrender to the power of the God Force, that's when things really begin to come together. Everything works better when God is involved. Perfect balance is powerful and all power is of God.

As a life coach, I have the privilege of helping individuals and organizations accomplish their goals and discover their Divine purpose in life. By focusing on the balance between body, mind and Spirit, you too can walk the path of light and become your highest gift. The end result will be a significant reduction in stress, greater clarity of purpose, and a higher quality of living. Just like riding a bike, once your life comes into balance, you will ride high in the saddle and wonder how in the world you ever lived any other way. Give these ideas a try and for crying out loud, be careful out there. I wouldn't want anyone to put their eye out!

Some Things To Consider

Think about your body, mind and spirit. What is the one thing you could do in each of those three areas that would move your life another step towards perfect balance? Begin doing those things this week. Repeat this procedure every week until perfect balance becomes a way of life for you.

To Share A Common Table

"No man is an island, entire of itself; every man is a piece of the continent, a part of the main; if a clod be washed away by the sea, Europe is the less, as well as if a promontory were, as well as if a manor of thy friends or of thine own were; any man's death diminishes, because I am involved in mankind; and therefore never send to know for whom the bell tolls; it tolls for thee"

John Donne

I seem to be much more tolerant these days, much more accepting of the beliefs and lifestyles of others. I no longer feel the need to *judge or define* anyone by his or her life-choices. I have begun to *see the oneness* that connects us all together. A oneness that is based on love rather than fear.

I much prefer to approach my earthly experience with an open-mind and accept others for who and what they are, not for who and what I would like them to be. I want to join them at *their* table and them at mine. I want to embrace our differences and respect our individual opinions. I want to understand *their* truth and listen more than I speak.

I don't think I am alone in this pursuit, for it suddenly feels that a spiritual resurgence is upon us. Every month, as I speak to various groups or exchange e-mail with those who have read my work, *I am refreshed and encouraged* by the spiritual changes that are beginning to take shape in our neighborhoods and around the planet. Could it be that our *collective souls are beginning to transform* the world in which we live?

We live in an age of rapid change, where what was once considered black and white and *the correct way to live,* is being challenged from every angle. The world no longer resembles—if it ever truly did—Father Knows

Best, Donna Reid or Leave It To Beaver. I think that's a good thing. After all, did anyone honestly believe that real people actually lived like that? Well, actually, we did. At least our parents did.

Those early television programs (and it's no coincidence they were in black and white) helped to establish and reinforce the role models and rules that would govern an entire generation. Rules, that for the most part, subjected us to someone else's standards and hid the truth about who we really were as spiritual beings. It was a time of cold war, racial violence and spiritual malnutrition, where, governed by fear and hatred, white Americans were taught to feel special—*distinct and different*—from all other human beings around the globe and even around our own cities. The social morays of the day divided us and pulled us apart. We learned to live by the rules and play the game, while at the same time starving for a one-on-one connection with the Devine.

Those were the days when we allowed rules (the ones that *we* created) to divide us as a country and put us on the dark road of separation as opposed to interdependence, love and light. These were the rules that allowed for racial segregation and the further refinement of a caste system, where one's social status and skin color allowed for certain privileges. These were the rules that drew lines in the sand and established a clear definition of the haves and the have-nots—rules that compared the world to football and eliminated any possibility of a *common table*. We indeed, saw ourselves as islands, disconnected from the whole of mankind. As a result, our spirituality as individuals and as a nation suffered. But, perhaps the tide has begun to turn…

As we have matured as a culture, we seem to have finally relaxed a little and become more comfortable with expressing the truth about who we are as spiritual beings. To the surprise of some, perhaps, our new-found truth is anything but black and white. While it may still be uncomfortable, it's no longer necessary to try to fit into someone else's belief system or remain in the closet regarding any area of our lives. More than ever before, each of us is free to step out and become our highest gift, whatever that gift may be.

The differences that once separated us now represent our greatest strength and promise for the future. The bridge that is being built, the connection that will ultimately allow us to fully accept each other, is based on love, spirit, compassion and tolerance. We are beginning to align ourselves not with rules but with our true purpose; not with what we think we should be but with who and what we truly are. The walls of social and religious conformity are beginning to come down.

In our own country for example, women are now free to be stay-at-home moms if they choose or run a Fortune 500 company. Men are free to make the *same* choice. Child rearing is no longer governed by a set of outdated rules based on gender, but rather on who has the ability and desire. Children will surely benefit from this honest and spirit filled approach.

The way we dress—long considered a social barometer—has taken on an unprecedented casualness, stemming from our *true desire* for comfortable clothing rather than from the (Madison Avenue created) need to wear what someone else may have defined as socially acceptable. In fact, the significance of clothing has dropped so far down the totem pole in the corporate world, that many companies are beginning to allow casual dress not only on Friday, but everyday of the week. It's no longer possible to clearly determine if someone is rich or poor simply by the clothes on their back. The affect has been neutralizing. Perhaps we're finally beginning to place more emphasis on ability rather than appearance, on talent as opposed to ties. I guess we've all had our fill of stuffed shirts…

Even the way we communicate with each other has changed dramatically, forcing us to *consider the message more than the messenger*. Take e-mail for example. When I receive e-mail from someone, I have no idea (unless they tell me) whether they are male or female, black or white, heterosexual or gay, rich or poor, Protestant, Catholic or New Age. All I can do (thank goodness) is consider the ideas they have expressed and choose my response accordingly without any prejudice or bias. The Internet has truly provided a *common table* where we can all come together and regardless of social status, race, gender or belief, exchange ideas in an open and honest forum.

Many of our spiritual masters have taught this great lesson—the lesson of namaste—and for the first time, perhaps, we are beginning to listen. *Namaste* means, "I will honor the place in you where we are all one." For example, some biblical scholars believe that the only reason Jesus infuriated the rulers of the day and was ultimately crucified, was simply because he had the nerve to sit at a *common table*. He saw no difference between the wife or the prostitute, the wealthy or the thief. He broke bread and shared His table with all of them. Jesus understood that we are all connected and He could see the presence of God in every person He met.

In another time and place, the teachings of the original Buddha consistently reinforced the notion that leaders should place themselves below that of their followers and not take pleasure in being honored. In fact, it was only after setting aside the material offerings of the prince, that Buddha became the bearer of the Buddha nature. "Do not look at the faults of others, or what one has done or not done; observe only what you yourself have done or not done." DHAMMAPADA 4.7

As I look at the issues facing our planet, from the unrest in the Middle East to the starvation in our country and around the world, to the violence in our schools, and the fear of terrorism, I am convinced more than ever that we must come together as one world and break bread at a *common table*. We must set aside our differences, embrace our diversity and celebrate the spiritual oneness that connects us all. We must see each other not as adversaries, but as spiritual beings sharing the same God and the same earthly experience. We must roll up our sleeves and begin to work together for a better world.

We seem to have spent so much time defining what it is we hate—what it is we are against—that we may have forgotten the magic that can occur the minute we change our focus to what it is we are for, what it is we love. It has been estimated that on the entire planet we spend approximately $25 million dollars every minute on the business of war and the ability to kill each other. During that very same minute, approximately forty children die of starvation. Do you think, that perhaps, we have our priorities a little twisted?

The world's playing field as well as the playing field within our own neighborhoods, is being leveled. No longer do we as Americans reign supreme in the global village called earth. We may have the majority of the money and the food, but we don't have the oil or the critical mass. Our weapons, which used to be our advantage, are now commonplace even among, what used to be considered, third world countries. In our own back yards, kids from affluent neighborhoods carry guns to school and take the lives of their fellow classmates just as kids in the inner cities have done for years.

No longer can we as individuals or as a nation, live in isolation simply because God has blessed us with a few more natural resources; simply because we think we're better. From a distance, in the eyes of God, we are all the same. To solve the world's problems, we need others as much as they need us.

Perhaps it's time we paused just long enough to let down our guard and recognize that we're all in this together. Perhaps it's time we confronted our fears and replaced those fears with love. Perhaps it's time we stopped seeing the world as black and white and got comfortable living *between the piano keys* where things are a little more gray, but much more honest. Perhaps it's time we began listening to one another and made a real effort to understand each other's truth. Perhaps it's time to *share a common table.*

Some Things To Consider

Spend the next week making a conscious effort to truly understand those who look, think, act or believe differently than you. If you're Christian, read from the Koran. If you're Muslim, read from the Bible. If you're neither, read from both. Seek to understand before you seek to be understood.

Nothing But The Truth, So Help Me God

"Honesty is such a lonely word,
everyone is so untrue."

Billy Joel

"Do you want me to tell the CEO the truth, or should I sugar-coat it?" Bill asked his boss Steve.

"Tell the old man what he wants to hear," Steve replied. "That's what I always do. He'll freak out if he knows how you really feel. Besides, we could both lose our jobs. Let's not take the risk."

"You're right," Bill said. "The last thing I want to do is ruin my career. I'll just package the truth like a bag of M&Ms. It'll taste so sweet he'll never know the real story. Thanks for the advice Steve."

What is it about telling the truth that frightens us? Are we so afraid of hurting someone's feelings that we would rather live a lie? Wouldn't it be healthier to express our true feelings, and let the chips fall where they may?

To answer these questions, it may be helpful to consider the oath we take before testifying in a court of law. As we raise our right hand, we promise to "tell the truth, the whole truth and nothing but the truth. So help us, God." Let's take a look at how this formula can be used to improve our daily lives.

- **Tell the truth.** We must first commit to telling the truth at all times, no matter what. No waffling on this one. We must make a pact with ourselves that in all situations we will express what we honestly feel to be our truth. This doesn't mean that we must force our truth on others, but it does mean that we will honestly express ourselves whenever our integrity is on the line or when not telling the truth might negatively effect another human being.

- **The whole truth.** This means a no-holds-barred approach. Everything that relates to our truth must be fully expressed. We often fall into the trap of expressing only partial truths in fear of how others will respond. We must express everything we feel without any attachment to the outcome. If someone *chooses* to respond negatively, that is their choice.

- **Nothing but the truth.** We must stick to the mission at hand. This is not a time to get sidetracked or attempt to manipulate the truth with our own hidden agenda. We must be honest with ourselves before speaking to make sure that our ego is not masquerading as truth. Tough assignment for most of us.

- **So help me, God.** This may be the most important part and often the one we forget. To express our truth without rancor or rage, without a hidden agenda or intent to harm, we must tap into God's loving guidance. God will empower us to express our truth at the right moment and in the right way, with courage, love and kindness. We might also ask ourselves how the great spiritual masters such as Jesus, Buddha or Mohammed, might express what we are about to say. Then we must *listen for the answer* as we pray or meditate. It **will** come.

Of all the things that God can bring to the expression of truth, love is by far the most important. Love is the ingredient that allows for our truth to be spoken in a manner that can be heard and accepted by others. If we are to express what we believe to be true, we must allow love to carry the message and allow God to bring love into the equation. God, love and truth are all interconnected. You cannot have one without the other two. Speak your truth with love, and trust God to handle the outcome.

Above all else in life, it seems that we must express and live our truth or resign ourselves to relationships that are false and phony. This includes our relationship with ourselves. Perhaps if each of us would find the courage to express our truth with love and kindness, honesty wouldn't have to be *such a lonely word* after all. As always, the choice is ours to make.

Some Things To Consider

Are there people in your life, including yourself, that perhaps you have not been totally honest with? Consider meeting with these people and clearing the air. If it's yourself, consider a long walk, some prayer or the sounding board of a trusted friend. Don't resign yourself to living among the false and phony. Embrace total honesty in all that you do and say.

NATURE'S SILENT TEAR

*"Life in the mountains is living in danger
of too many people too many machines."*
John Denver

I have often found the hidden meanings of life and all of its wonderful blessings while hiking across nature's leathery face—in the deep crevasses that make up her laugh lines or the foot paths and worn arteries that wind through her soul. Seemingly moving to my own rhythm, I am reminded that I am but a cog in the movement of all mankind. In these times of bliss, nature teaches me that we are all connected in a oneness that was here well before our eyes ever caught the first glimpse of her radiant beauty. The presence of nature and all she gives to us is the power that lives in us all.

These moments can come with a revelation as loud and as noticeable as the crack of thunder as it echoes through the canyons or softly whispered to us using a secret code carried in the wind and manifested in the form of recently opened wild flowers. Nature can and will flood our consciousness with raindrops of truth and serenity if we are but wise enough to grant her passage into our lives.

We often take it for granted, this beauty, this nature. We race through life without taking time to notice what has been provided for us, until of course it is taken away—stripped from our consciousness like a child who loses a toy.

When I gaze at the majestic and understand that I am but a passenger in this wonder, I allow myself to absorb all the beauty and grace that has been given to me—free of charge—no strings attached. I can lay at rest all my concerns about tomorrow and just focus on a tiny blade of grass, a western sunset or the clean crisp air flowing through my lungs. Nature cleanses me from a multitude of sins. Nature makes me whole again.

I am but a visitor in this world that animals call home. An unwanted guest in the living room of the wild places, where man has forced his presence at the risk of destroying it all. I tread gently on this turf and pray that my intrusion upon this magical place will be as unnoticed as footprints on pine needles or wind on sand.

I am grateful to be part of this beauty, if only as a bystander awash in a musical repertoire of songs written from the heart of God. I seek to understand its meaning, knowing full well that it may not be mine to know. But I am comfortable with the unknowing, the blind journey, for it is there that I find the curious contentment of a thirst quenched, a soul saved.

Driven with a desire to connect to the rivers and streams that flow abundant with the history of my existence, I as a human being, reach out for need of nothing but seemingly want for everything. In return, I am given the gift of abundance and knowledge and truth—nature will and does provide in ways often unseen. I touch her face with gentleness and caress the beauty that lies at my feet…

It is, without warning, that the trance is broken—the dream shattered—the truth revealed. Just up ahead in a clearing, obscured by dark shadows and the awful stench of something dying, the machinery can be seen—the sound of destruction can be heard. The cuts, the scars, the bleeding—deep wounds made to the earth's surface by greedy men with visions of shopping malls and track housing. Everyday stealing just a little more, just another piece from what was once untouched and serene. A cry for help rings out from the forest from all of those with hoofed feet or majestic wings—the earth speaks to those we think cannot, those who were here first. A silent tear is shed but goes unnoticed by the vast majority of humans, those with better things to do.

Because of our ignorance and false need to improve what is already perfect, we have begun to take away the only reference we have to heaven on earth—God's original work of art—the wonderful tranquility and awesome beauty of nature. The machines of destruction rage on ripping our mother earth apart—while we look the other way, focused on corporate profits, quickly calculating how many more homes can be built and sustained with the water that remains in her veins. We rape her repeatedly and leave her to die. My knees weaken. My stomach turns. The thought of it all leaves me gagging with self-disgust.

For the first time I realize that my own lack of involvement has allowed this tragedy to happen. I and all of my brothers and sisters who share in what nature has bestowed upon us, have allowed those among us who would steal our precious resources, to destroy the peace and make war with the earth. We pretend we do not see the laws that are written, the handshakes—eyes winking—as deals are cut, money exchanged. Our ignorance is fuel for the fire that seeks to burn down and destroy the vast mountain wilderness we call our home.

Will this be the legacy our generation will leave to our children? How far will we let it go? How long will it continue before we realize enough is enough? The heavy equipment continues to cut a path of destruction through our forests at alarming rates while we look on as if we have no other choice than to let the bleeding continue. But we do have a choice. We can make a difference.

Of all the tears we've cried in our life times—tears of joy, tears of sorrow, tears of pain—perhaps it is time to shed a tear that matters. One that can be heard as it extinguishes the flames that seek to destroy what is only ours to borrow. A tear that says, " We will no longer stand by and watch as the mountains are leveled, the air polluted, the water contaminated, nature destroyed." Extinction is indeed forever. The time to act is now.

Some Things To Consider

Get outside and take a hike through the forest. Find a quiet place, be still and just notice the world around you. Notice any animals that might be near by and watch as they go about *their* day. Breathe deeply and pay attention to the scent of the trees and the fragrance of the flowers. If it's winter, embrace the beauty of the snow and see if you can hear it as it falls from the sky and kisses the ground. Now, make a pact with yourself that you will begin doing this at least once a week, every week, for the rest of your life.

From Frequent Flyer To Frequent Father

*"Every father should remember that one day
his son will follow his example instead of his advice."*

Unknown

The earth-shattering news arrived on Saturday afternoon, just as I was preparing to take my newborn son on a short hike outside my home in the Rocky Mountains. I tore open the plain brown envelope, whose small letters suggested it had been printed on recycled paper, only to find a very serious message from the president of a major airline. As I read the letter I found myself laughing at the following words, written in a tone of sorrow, as if someone had died:

"We regret to inform you, that, due to the reduced number of air miles you flew with us last year, we must downgrade your platinum frequent flyer status."

What? How could it be? With the stroke of a pen I had been reduced from top-of-the-heap to lowest-on-the-totem pole! Cut down in my prime. No longer a player. What would I do? I shuddered to think what the future might hold!

In the world of business travel, one's frequent-flyer card is a coveted status symbol, much like one's income level or corporate title. Possessing the top-level card means you are considered a *mover and shaker*— someone who makes things happen as you circle the globe.(Not to mention the fact that you get to board first, while other less-fortunate souls must wait until

83

your butt is comfortably seated before they are allowed to find a home for their carry-on luggage.)

When I gave up the corporate world several years ago, I said goodbye to the road—a place I called home for the better part of my adult life. My wife and I decided to start our family after 16 years of marriage, something that is difficult to do if you're never in the same house, let alone the same room, at the same time. But I happily parted ways with the friendly skies. No regrets.

Our son was born last year, and, since then, life has changed considerably. My fast-paced world of airlines and rental cars has been reduced to a 20-second daily commute from my bedroom to my in-home office. Power lunches at chic restaurants have given way to dining at home with our little toddler, who often attempts to turn graham crackers into some sort of a *mud facial.* As unglamorous as this may seem, I'm around to watch my son grow up. Something I wouldn't trade for a <u>million </u>frequent-flyer points!

What has changed most, however, is my deep understanding that to be a good father you *have to be available and involved.* Losing my frequent-flyer status has come to represent what I have gained rather than what I have given up. Here are just a few lessons that this new Frequent Father and former frequent-flyer has taken to heart:

- Frequent-flyer points are simply a measurement of how often you are away from your family. When it comes to the growth and development of your children, the lower your frequent-flyer status, the better. When the airline says, "You're out of the club," that's great! Now you can join a far more important—and somewhat obscure—club: parents who spend time with their kids.
- For me, staying in the finest hotel in the world is no match for holding my son in my arms and kissing him good night—every night. When Josh buries his head in my chest and gives me a hug, the feeling is priceless. Free turndown service or a chocolate on my pillow doesn't even come close!

- Becoming actively involved as a parent is far more rewarding than any free vacation you might earn with frequent-flyer points. When you're at 32,000 feet racking up the miles for that "free trip," your son or daughter is on the ground wondering if you'll return in time to help with tomorrow's spelling test.

If, like many parents, you must travel for a living, I certainly don't discount the sacrifices you're making to provide a better life for your family. But, the next time you begin to think that the frequent-flyer points you're earning are part of that "better life," think again. Treating your family to a free vacation in the south of France is no substitute for the many hours you're away from home. Priceless family time, once lost, is gone forever.

Among frequent flyers, there's a well known joke: He with the most points when he dies, wins! That's a game *this reformed road warrior* fully intends to lose.

Some Things To Consider

How much time are you spending with the ones you love? Can you find a way to spend more? What will it cost? Can the price ever be too high?

FOR THIS, I AM GRATEFUL

"There are two kinds of gratitude: the sudden kind we feel for what we take; and the larger kind we feel for what we give."

E.A. Robinson

There is often much to complain about. In a world seemingly gone mad, the bitter often stands tall in a forest of the sweet. We seem *forever focused* on what is wrong with our lives or constantly preoccupied with that which has yet to take place. In doing so, we set ourselves up for living in a constant state of complaining. Complaining about things that haven't gone our way, people that don't behave as we would like them to, and a world that just isn't quite perfect enough to meet our expectations. Our habitual focus on what is wrong blinds us from all that is right.

Negative attitudes can be contagious. In fact, the negativity of only one person can sway the entire mood of a group. One person begins to expound upon all that is wrong and the next thing you know, everyone gets pulled into the negative energy pattern. Before you can say, "slit my wrist" *the whoa-is-me* syndrome begins to feed upon itself. Suddenly, everyone is fueling the fire because misery truly does love company.

But nothing good ever comes from complaining because a negative attitude never leads or even follows—it only gets in the way. When all is said and done, much has been said but nothing has been done. Negativity can suck the life out of living and kill our dreams before they ever get off the launching pad. But it doesn't have to be that way.

The flip side of complaining is to be grateful for the *many* blessings that have been bestowed upon us. To graciously acknowledge all that is good and right with our lives. To give thanks for all that has been given to us, rather than fixating on that which we do not yet have.

Living in a state of gratitude quiets the desires of the ego and allows us to enter a state of bliss. We become content with what we have—with just being—and no longer feel the need to acquire more things, more stuff. Rather than striving, we feel as if we have arrived. There is an inner peace, a conscious *knowing,* that *where we are is right where we're suppose to be.*

Gratitude leads to a life of service. Because when we begin to give thanks for all that we have, we can begin to give of ourselves to others in a way that we may never have experienced before. This outward expression of love and kindness, can lead us to improve the world around us and ultimately free our souls for a life of contribution. For in many ways, the expression of gratitude is an extension of love and every act of love sets us free.

By giving thanks everyday for the many wonderful things that touch our lives, we set ourselves up to expect only *good* things from others. By focusing on all that is just and true, it is difficult to get caught up in negativity. This approach can allow us to contribute to the world in a positive way, because rather than simply *faking* a positive attitude, we are honestly feeding our psyche with the things that we are truly grateful for. And believe me, when you really start to consider all that is right with your life, it is all but impossible to feel anything but positive! A positive attitude begins with abundant gratitude.

The next time you're feeling down and ready to complain about all that is wrong, try this exercise. Rise early in the morning, long before anyone else. Find a comfortable chair, preferably somewhere where you can watch the sunrise. (By the way, how long has it been since you've seen a sunrise? In all its magnificent beauty, a sunrise, more than anything else, symbolizes a fresh start and a new beginning. It's a great way to start the day!)

Simply begin by giving thanks to God for all that you are grateful for. Don't be concerned with how you say it—just say it. Give thanks for anything and everything that comes to mind. Your list might be very different from that of someone else, or remarkably similar in many ways. That being said, here are a few things that I am grateful for. I offer them here as merely a starting point, as you seek your own path to gratitude.

1) **God.** As my source of strength and inspiration, the power of God lives within me just as it lives within everything in the universe. In my darkest moments, this power has allowed me to transcend the ways of the world and release my spirit to higher levels of being. I surrender to this power and allow it to fill my life with unconditional love.

2) **Family.** Blessed with a child just a few short years ago, I have found a wonderful sense of direction that I never had before. My family continues to teach me the meaning of love—a definition that expands each and every day. I am also grateful for the two people who gave me life—my parents.

3) **Friends.** My life is abundant with the gift of friendship. My closest friends are as different and unique as snowflakes. On any given weekend, we break bread and enjoy each other's company as we share our unique experience of this thing called life. I am grateful for the good times we share and I pray I never take them for granted.

4) **Health.** Be grateful if you are blessed with good health. Consider it a gift and think of ways you can help those less fortunate. Jesus washed the feet of his disciples and we can do the same in our own lives. Pay close attention to those who are sick and reach out and help them in your own unique way. Be a servant to those in need.

The funny thing about gratitude is that the more you give the more you get. What we think about expands and so it is that as you rise each morning to give thanks for all that is right in your life, your list of all that you are grateful for will continue to grow and grow. I pray that you will use this new found sense of well being to create a greater sense of purpose. By working to improve your life and the lives of those around you, you will ultimately create, in your own small way, a better world. And that is something we will all be grateful for.

Some Things To Consider

What are you grateful for in your life? List the people, places and things that bring you joy. Send them love through meditation and prayer. Begin each day by giving thanks for these blessings and add to the list as time goes on.

No Regrets

*"The nearer our time comes for our departure from this life,
the greater our regret for wasting so much of it."*

Unknown

"She lived a life of no regrets," the pastor said.

I left the funeral with vivid memories of Dorothy, my old college professor, running like a movie through my head. I thought about it—the "no regrets" part—the part that spoke of all she had done with her long productive life. A life that seemed like three lifetimes when compared to the accomplishments of her peers.

Dorothy Clayton was always involved. She would jump in with both feet to take on a humanitarian task or simply tie a child's shoelace when other equally concerned citizens were content to be, well, concerned. You would never see her waiting around for the right time or the right place or the right emotion to overtake her. She simply did what she felt life demanded of her right then and there and saw it through to completion. She once remarked "Life offers too many second chances to ever have any regrets." She took advantage of every second chance that came along.

Her passion and zest for living stayed with her well into her eighties. In the five years before her death she took up skydiving, sang in a barbershop quartet, went scuba diving at the Great Barrier Reef, traveled Europe, met the prime minister of England and taught her grandchildren to write poetry. She even found the time to finish writing another book—her personal memoirs—something she had started thirty-five years earlier. Said she stuck it on the backburner until all her academic writing was done. Regrets? Doubtful. A full life? Absolutely.

Why is it that so many of us have regrets? How is it possible to be among the living, perhaps as young as thirty, forty or fifty, wishing we had done something that we have yet to do and feel as if we will never do it? If we define regrets as something we should have done but haven't yet, can't we still do it? Why have we given up?

By choosing to *regret*, we have in essence, given up on what it is we truly want. After all, we would never regret something unless it was very important to us. Things that are unimportant are never regretted, they are simply forgotten. But regrets carry a very different meaning in our lives. These are things we have determined to be crucial—things that really matter—things we really want and most importantly *need* to accomplish in our *lifetime*.

The word lifetime means *time for life*—a connected stretch of moments when we are given the opportunity to manifest our souls in physical form. Its length unknown, its direction our choice, this thing called life begins as quite a *surprise* to us as we poke our heads out of the womb for the first time. Life then continues until we are *surprised* once again by death. We never really know for sure how long we will live.

In this *time for life* between birth and death, we are each given an unknown amount of time to figure out and then go about *doing* our life's mission. Since we can't say for sure how long we will be on earth, it seems absurd to regret anything, since we may very well have plenty of time left to act upon the desires of our heart. But instead, we often take ourselves out of the game when success was just around the corner.

Regrets, like many other things, reflect our level of courage and belief in ourselves at the moment of choice. If we look back and proclaim that we regret having done or not having done something, we are in truth making a statement about the decisions we have made. But those are the decisions of our past and cannot be replayed. However, by learning from the past and listening to our hearts desire, our present moments can be a wonderful journey as we seek to bring our dreams into reality.

Here's a few more thoughts on *regrets*:

- **The freedom of aging.** Many of us begin to think life is over somewhere around our 40th birthday. We are no longer youthful in appearance; our hair is thinning, our waistlines expanding. It seems as if nature has played a dirty trick on us so we frantically try to recapture our youth. We dye our hair, leave our spouse for someone younger and seemingly more attractive, or buy that hot sports car we always wanted. But it's all a big lie that will continue to rob us of our energy as long as we buy into the fallacy that we need to remain youthful. Turn the tables and realize that the second half of your life can be the best half because you no longer need to waste time and energy playing the game of youth! You can now *choose* to become the person you were always meant to be. The writer, the musician, the artist, the whatever. It's all within your reach. Start slowly but take a step each day that brings you closer to the real you—perhaps *the you* you've kept silent all these years.

- **Remove the roadblocks.** Determine what it is you want to do and then remove the obstacles that stand in the way of your goal. For most of us, the biggest roadblock is finding the *time* to do what we really want to do. The solution in most cases is to simply say no to the urgent and yes to the important. In other words, get rid of the time wasters—people and things that try to steal your precious time. Once done, fill those spaces with what is really important to you. And for heavens sake, don't worry about what others may think—the biggest roadblock of all!

- **See what can still be.** The minute you slap the label of regret on something, you give up on ever doing it. "I regret never becoming a dancer," my dear friend Susan said as she blew out the candles on her 65th birthday cake. In the corner of the room sat a dusty catalog of summer activities offered by the local college. Dance lessons were part of the curriculum. Susan never saw it because regret had taken away her ability to see what could still be. She lived another 20 years and never found the time to dance. She died with her music still inside her.

- **Begin.** Procrastination can kill most dreams before they ever get off the ground. Once you know what it is you want to do, START DOING IT! Let's say you want to play piano. The minute you take your first piano lesson, you have become a pianist—albeit not a very proficient one yet—but a pianist nonetheless. Just take the first baby step and the rest will follow.

- **Drop your pride.** Perhaps what you really regret most is not having said "I'm sorry" or "I love you" to an important person in your life. Are they still among the living? Want to feel a whole lot better? Go do it now. Sure, it's possible your apology won't be accepted or that your love might be rejected, but at least you will feel better knowing you tried to add more peace and love to the world. Too much pride can prevent you from doing many things in your life—get rid of it now!

In my own life I have made many blunders. I have said things in the past that I surely would not say today and done things that I would never dream of doing again. I have offended others with the power of the written word and spoke with uncontrolled hatred and anger. But I can honestly say that I have no regrets about the things I've done. Why? Because I have apologized for my mistakes, try not to repeat them and I know that the past is just that—past. It is over and done with. It cannot be relived.

I do have regrets however, about the things I didn't do. Things that my heart told me were important—my own personal truth that I chose, for the sake of convenience or the presence of fear, to ignore. I plan to revisit those desires that resonate so deeply within my soul. I plan to take action, put fear aside and go after the truth of my heart. I pray you will do the same.

Some Things To Consider

Are there things in your life that still need to be done? Does it bother you knowing that you may never do them? These are your future regrets.

Make a list of all these things and begin doing them one by one. You don't have to do them all at once, just start chipping away at them. You will be amazed at how much better you will feel just knowing that you are working on the important areas of your life—even if its just a few baby steps in the right direction.

River Of Souls

"Of all the options available, a life focused on helping others—on giving ver-sus taking—is of the highest magnitude. Our own soul and the souls of others are greatly enriched the more we contribute to the betterment of mankind."

Jeffrey Alan Hall

The phone rang with the intensity of an air-raid siren, shooting adren-aline through my entire body and forcing me from a deep sleep. I reached in the dark for the receiver, knocking the lamp from the nightstand—the cat sprang to her feet in a flourish of activity that was certain to cause her cardiac arrest.

It's Saturday, I thought. Who on earth would be calling at 5:30 in the morning?

"Let's ride to the top of Bergen Peak," the voice on the phone exclaimed as I untangled the cord and turned the mouthpiece from my ear to its proper position. "It's supposed to be in the high 80s; a beautiful Colorado day. Let's do it!"

It was Emily. With her cancer now in remission, phone calls like this one were becoming the norm.

Tears of joy began to wash the *sand* from my tired eyes as I thought about the spiritual transformation that had recently taken place in her life—a transformation that had left her doctors scratching their heads and Emily scratching to live the life she was meant to live. She had beaten the poison of cancer, for now at least. But, as she was so fond of saying, "Now is all we ever get."

"Sounds good to me," I said, as the words "mind over mattress" went round and round in my head. "I'll meet you in an hour."

All my senses rejoiced in the beauty of a *newborn mountain day* as we lifted our bikes from their rooftop carriers and began to prepare for the 2,000-foot ascent. I had just locked in one toe clip and was about to swing my other leg over the saddle when Emily approached me with wide-eyed jubilation.

"I have to tell you about my meditation this morning," she said. "Once again, God spoke to me offering both strength and hope. It's apparent to me now that I still have a good deal more to contribute. It's clear that my time here on earth is not up yet. You have to hear this, Jeffrey! God has a lot to say!"

Emily had attributed her success in the battle against cancer to the *spiritual awakening* that had so profoundly changed her life. On many occasions during the past several months, she had shared with me the revelations that God had made known to her—revelations, that I knew, must be captured and written down.

As the morning sun began to peek its head over the mountains, Emily began to speak and I began to write…

> *"Life on earth is replenished over and over again by an ever-flowing river of souls. All around us, souls can be seen arriving and departing as they manifest themselves into physical form, live their physical life and then return once again to be embraced in the arms of God. Each and every soul will have eternal life. Death need not be feared.*
>
> *Each soul chooses when to arrive on earth. Once here, free will allows each soul to choose how it will manifest itself and create the physical reality it desires based on the lessons it came to learn. Of all the options available, a life focused on helping others—on giving versus taking—is of the highest magnitude. Our own soul and the souls of others are greatly enriched the more we contribute to the betterment of mankind.*

Nothing is coincidental. Other souls arrive in our lives at just the right moment. As the student is ready, the teacher will appear, reaching out in his or her own way to enrich and improve the spiritual walk of the student. This is the meaning of life—our magnificent mission—to teach what we know and to learn what we do not. It is within this environment of mutual trust and respect that the possibility of heaven on earth exists.

The energy source of the soul is love, though it is often confused with fear. You will always know that you are "on purpose" and fulfilling your life's mission, when love is what drives you. The difference is quite clear; Love will propel you, fear will prevent you. Love manifests itself through giving, while fear manifests itself through taking. Love pulls towards, while fear pushes away.

Souls look very similar as the river brings them into and out of this physical life. That is why babies and the elderly often resemble each other physically. Our skin, our hair and even our teeth, manifest as the soul enters the earth plane, but are no longer of any use as a soul reaches the end of its physical life and prepares to return to God. In the spiritual world, nothing physical is required.

Religious differences, as well as those of skin color, are but two of the many lessons that souls have come to earth to learn. But these lessons alone have had a more profound effect on the human experience than any other. Many a war has been fought over race and religion. All such wars will continue to manifest themselves until this lesson has been learned: All souls are connected by love to the same body, the same God Force. Hurting another hurts all of mankind. Just as you would not put out your own eye or cut off your own arm, nor should you harm one another.

The power of love should never be underestimated. What we have come to know as love, is the ultimate connection of souls at the deepest level. As souls connect in this way, their ability to influence the physical lives of other souls becomes greatly increased. This is why the Bible and other great spiritual works speak of the idea that there is love where "two or more are gathered." The collective power and energy of souls connected by love, can light a thousand cities and improve the quality of life for all of mankind.

Finally, understand that contribution to the greater good has nothing to do with size or scale. Many people think they must contribute to the universe in some grand way or their time on earth will have been for naught. This is not necessarily true. Look for little ways in your own world to make life better for others, and use the gifts God has given you. The fruits of your labor may not be immediately apparent to you, but that should not cause you worry. Focus only on the doing, not on the outcome."

As the lesson ended, we mounted our bikes and headed for the summit. We arrived at the top of Bergen Peak, physically exhausted but spiritually nourished. During the entire ride I thought about all that Emily had said that morning. She had touched me in ways I had never known before. I now recognized that she was teaching me some of the very lessons that my soul had come to earth to learn. Lessons, that until now, I had overlooked. The student was ready. The teacher appeared.

Some Things To Consider

How is God speaking to you? What is the God force saying? The first step towards hearing God speak in your life is simply to believe that it can happen. God didn't stop speaking to us a couple of thousand years ago. He, She, It speaks to each of us 24/7. How often do you take the time to listen?

LOVE

"And in the end, the love you take,
Is equal to the love you make"
Lennon-McCartney

Love is everything. We are born into this world to give love to each other. Love flows from person to person in a circular fashion as we each bestow upon the life of another, unconditional love. Like the sound of fresh snow falling in a quiet forest, I believe that life was meant to be just that simple and pure. Love is part of each of us. It was placed in our hearts at conception. We carry it with us for all of eternity.

The innocence that accompanied our souls on their spiritual journey from nowhere to now-here, was born of a deep and everlasting love that serves as a reminder of what life on earth would be like if love were allowed to prevail. The capacity to love and to use love for the betterment of the world is a gift we can all partake of and share with each other no matter what our station in life. We are each called to minister the spirit of love to each other in our own unique way. It is our sole purpose for existing. There cannot be a more noble pursuit.

We seem to struggle with the possibility that life can really be that simple—that love is all we need to know. We distort and complicate the whole idea of love, desperately searching to find meaning among the meaningless. We buy things—lots of things—expensive things—believing that in some way they will fill the void and make us happy. They do not.

When we give our love in this way—to the materialistic as opposed to the spiritual—our love never has the chance to fully blossom. When we love the meaningless we are never truly satisfied because that which is of the material world can never love us back. Our love flows from our hearts to an object and then stops dead in its tracks. The circle is broken.

Our constant focus on finding love outside ourselves has lead many of us to believe that the world is a rather loveless place. We never find the love we are so desperately seeking because we only focus our attention on what the world has to offer. Because the world cannot fulfill our needs, we believe that love does not exist. But the world it seems is the last place we should be looking for love. For as Jesus and other spiritual masters teach us, true love can only be found within ourselves as we pursue the realm of the spiritual and seek a one-on-one relationship with God. Only then will we ever be truly satisfied and fulfilled.

Love is a source of energy that can drive the human spirit and illuminate the world. It cannot be seen with the naked eye but can only be felt by the human heart. It is the power that God gives to us unconditionally—no strings attached—in hopes that we will in turn release our love upon the world through the unselfish giving of our time and talents to others. The power of love can only be fully realized when it is allowed to be unleashed and freely given away. It is the giving that makes the difference. Kept hidden within ourselves, love serves no useful purpose.

Think about the times in your life when you have been most at peace. Think about how it felt and what caused those moments of bliss. Chances are, it was the giving of love to another human being or the comforting of a soul in a time of need that brought about your own sense of well-being. That's the magic of it all. Love returns to our lives in abundance as we give more and more of it away.

It is never hate or anger that allows us to feel our lives are on purpose, that our mission is being fulfilled. In fact, anger and hate have quite the opposite effect. Whenever we hate or point blame or allow our egos to dominate our existence, the world seems false, phony and obscene. We are fearful, miserable and void of inner peace. We lose our sense of trust in others and ourselves. Our lives are off center. Our potential diluted.

Deep down inside, I believe each of us understands that love is the only way out—the only solution for a world gone seemingly mad. Each of us shares the knowledge—at some deep spiritual level—that in order to be truly fulfilled, truly alive, we must let love and nothing else dominate our lives. We know that when we operate from love we are happy, content and at peace with the universe. So why do we fight it? Why is it so hard, so seemingly uncomfortable, to simply take our hands off the handle bars and let love direct us? Perhaps the answer lies in our ego and its relentless need for control.

For many people, riding on the back of a motorcycle can be a rather frightening experience. It's uncomfortable to surrender control and perhaps your own safety to someone other than yourself. Our ego wants to be the one doing the steering—the one in charge—the one calling the shots with regards to our life. Seems natural, right?

But that same ego—the one that fears losing control—is what holds us back from surrendering ourselves to the power of love. Yet, surrendering is exactly what we must do if we are to ever find peace and allow love to dictate the direction of our lives. Just as a flower will blossom or a river will flow without any help from us, love too has a power all its own. We need only surrender to this power and allow the seed to be planted in our lives. Love will do the rest.

For most of us, surrendering to anything or anyone is something we're just not comfortable with—it feels like failure. After all, when was the last time anything of value was ever won by surrendering? In our culture, winning is often everything and to win we must never surrender. But love wears a different game face. Love isn't something we need to win, it is simply something we need to embrace.

Love stands waiting at the doorstep of our lives seeking an entrance through open wounds. To surrender to it, is to let the power come in and heal us. Nothing else can fill the void in our hearts. Nothing else will complete us. Only love can make us whole.

To borrow a line from an old song, it seems that many of us have been "looking for love in all the wrong places". We search for it in the romantic eyes of another human being, in the accumulation of worldly possessions or in the ideas of false idols and teachers. Many of us think we need to improve ourselves in order to be worthy of love. That somehow we are inadequate and not already perfect. We look everywhere for love except the one place that held the answer all along—God.

We resist the need to just let Go(d). In fact, many of us often spend a good deal of our lives refusing to believe that there could be a higher power that controls the universe. We want to be in charge. We want to be our own God; masters of our own destiny. We agree with Sinatra; we want to do it "Our Way". But more times than we care to admit (especially us baby boomers) our way often involves the use of alcohol, sex, drugs and other escape mechanisms that work for the moment but fail us in the long run. Hey, remember the 70's? I don't.

As our lives spin further and further out of control, we reach out for a higher truth. It is at that point that many of us hand our lives over to God, surrendering to the power of love. Where we once felt secure in the false knowledge that we were in control, it is now quite comforting to know that we are not. We allow love to take control and illuminate our lives with a peace we have never known before. We begin to understand that love must be our destination and the only way to get there is through God. When our lives or the lives of our beloved are hanging in the balance, there can be no greater truth.

There is a passage in the Bible so eloquently written, so positively beautiful, that it could only have come from the voice of God. It is the truest description, I think, of what love is meant to be. It reads " *Love is very patient and kind, never jealous or envious, never boastful or proud, never haughty or selfish or rude. Love does not demand its own way. It is not irritable or touchy. It does not hold grudges and will hardly ever notice when others do it wrong. It is never glad about injustice but rejoices whenever truth wins out.*"

During this holiday season, I pray that each of us allows the love that so defines this time of year, to expand in our lives and continue to mold and shape our earthly experience each and every day. That somehow we will see as a people, as a nation and as a world that love is our only hope. That love is all that matters. That love is all we are and all we were ever meant to be.

Some Things To Consider

Spend an entire day freely giving love away to others—no strings attached. Just give unconditional love to each and everyone you come into contact with for the next 24 hours—the checkout person at the grocery store, the bank teller, the plumber, your life partner, your family, your pet—everyone!

No matter what happens, just send them love. At the end of the day, note how it made you feel. Note how it made them feel. Do it again next week. Or better yet—tomorrow!

Pastor Denny, Halloween and The War Against Evil

"No, thanks. I don't believe in evil. Don't convince me. I don't want to believe. The belief in evil is a dangerous thing. It promotes attack and counter attack. If we hope to create anything different, we must start with some other assumption."

John Cowan

"It's Halloween my friends and we are fighting a battle against the devil," pastor Denny angrily exclaimed from his television pulpit. "Right versus wrong, light versus darkness. There are those among us—witches—who celebrate Halloween as a religious holiday. We must take this *very* seriously. We must win the war against evil!"

Before I could find the remote control to change channels or at least hit the mute button, the good pastor—with very bad hair—identified, what looked like a sick and desperate woman, barely able to walk to the stage. At that very moment, an invisible source of power appeared to shoot from pastor Denny's index finger directly into the ailing woman, immediately knocking her from her feet—her body jolting from side to side as if some-one had just yelled "clear!" and applied electrodes to her chest. Now grin-ning from ear to ear the woman rose from the floor as the good pastor and *self-proclaimed general* in the war against evil, pronounced her "cured" of her illness—right there on my TV!

"Ladies and gentlemen," pastor Denny continued, "I have just attacked and eliminated evil from this poor women's body. She has been healed! Do I hear an *Amen*!

The audience cheered with all the passion of an Amway meeting. Emotional music began to play. Men carrying large buckets began to *collect money* from the now dazed flock of followers; many who looked as if they had recently received a prefrontal lobotomy. I sat there—fully expecting to see a snake oil advertisement—while carving a face on a pumpkin and wondering if my recent purchase of a satellite dish antenna was such a good idea after all.

And the woman? Oh, she was healed all right—well heeled, I would surmise. It's anybody's guess how much they paid this actress for her 15 seconds of fame. Whatever amount it was, I am sure it was worth every penny—just the cost of doing business in the *war against evil*. I changed channels thinking Dan Rather might be a safer bet.

Through a constant parade of trick-or-treaters in search of their annual sugar buzz, I watched the news with the *concept of evil* (thanks to Pastor Denny) rolling around in my mind. I saw plenty of dangerous people— some adults, some children—many who had committed heinous crimes. Aha! These must be the evil people pastor Denny was speaking of, I thought. But as the newscast continued, I wasn't so sure.

By the time Dan signed off, I actually felt some compassion for these so-called "evil people". I realized that they certainly were not demon possessed, but rather had an improper and distorted view of the world and their place in it. A little like, well, Pastor Denny, I thought. I answered the door to find a vampire standing there, dropped a candy bar in his bag and pondered the thought…

Labeling something as *evil* has long been a powerful tool for many opportunistic religious zealots, in that it gives them something broad, ambiguous and undefined to be against. It allows them *to point their finger* at something they feel must be stopped—a blurred focal point by which to rally the troops and make it acceptable *to destroy the evil* they are so sure they have found. Hatred becomes part of the doctrine—part of the brainwashing. The tactic is as old as mankind itself.

Over the centuries, well-meaning followers who believe they have seen evil in the face of the enemy have waged many a war. Northerners fought the Southerners. The white man fought the red man. Church denominations fight each other. I can even recall an old friend claiming, during a heated argument, that he *saw the fiery eyes of the devil in the face of another human being*. That human being was me. Fortunately, the finger he pointed at me that night (not his index finger!) was as powerless as pastor Denny's!

There are many things in this world that I personally detest—war, hatred, racism and cancer, to name just a few. These things take away from the quality of life we all equally deserve. In many ways, they are the very opposite of what is good, just and true. In many ways they are things that can be very damaging to mankind. But by placing them in that big black hole called *evil,* we eliminate any possibility for understanding what may be at the heart of the problem. We eliminate any possibility for rolling up our sleeves and *working to find a solution*. We waste our time by seeking to destroy something that never existed to begin with.

Everything in the universe is the result of unconditional love—the energy of the God Force. God created *everything* with the energy of love. Nothing exists that was not created by the God Force; hence, nothing exists that was not created by love. Evil, as a power, cannot exist because love (God) would not have created it. Thus, evil as we know it, is a man-made creation. It is a product of our clever and fearful egos and as such, does not exist in the world of spirit but *only in the world of the mind*.

You see, our egos want us to believe in evil, because by doing so, our attention and focus gets placed on *something outside ourselves*. By believing in evil, we don't have to accept responsibility for the bad choices we make, we can simple blame it on the devil or some other figment of our imaginations. Evil becomes the ultimate scapegoat.

Recently, while on a flight from Denver to LA, I sat next to a medical doctor who is actively involved in the battle against AIDS. After the usual small talk required of two strangers suddenly occupying a space the size of a broom closet, I asked him what his greatest challenge was.

"Dollars," he quickly replied. " Because of the *evil stigma* attached to this disease, we have a very difficult time securing the necessary funding desperately needed for research. You see, many people are comfortable writing checks to fight MS or cystic fibrosis but because they see AIDS and everything attached to it *as evil,* they feel justified looking the other way and refusing to help."

"But what is truly evil," he passionately continued, "Is the sad fact that if we only had more funding, much more could be done to save those who are dying each and everyday. It's time to stop calling AIDS the *evil disease,* and start working overtime to find a cure."

I shook my head in agreement. I knew that he was right.

I have no doubt that I will continue to see the *war against evil* being aggressively fought by pastor Denny and many just like him on my TV screen every Sunday morning. I have no doubt that countless followers will blindly pledge their allegiance and dollars to support "the cause". I only wish the enemy actually had a face. But, then again, maybe—reflecting back through the mirror in pastor Denny's dressing room—it does.

Some Things To Consider

Are there problems in your life that you have not addressed because you have placed them in that big black hole called *evil?* Consider for a moment that evil does not exist. Now look at those problems again and think about the appropriate steps that need to be taken to solve them. Enlist the help of others if you need to but come up with an action plan that you can implement within the next week.

The Power Of Words

"Words that enlighten the soul are more precious than jewels."
Hazrat Inayat Khan

"I think I can! I think I can! I think I can!" The Little Train That Thought It Could coughed out an endless trail of black smoke as it strained to inch its way up a long and steep hill, entertaining me for the moment and leaving a lasting impression that would affect me for the rest of my life. I was only four or five when Captain Kangaroo introduced me to that little train; my first motivational seminar I suppose. Yet, some forty years later, whenever I am faced with a difficult challenge, I still draw upon those words for inspiration. Silly, but true…

Ever wonder why people turn out the way they do? Why some will climb mountains achieving great things, while others remain at base camp, with frozen desires, afraid of taking a step forward? Given all the options we have in this life, all the wonderful possibilities of how we could best use our time and talents, why is it that some of us live our dreams while others let them pass by?

I think a lot of it has to do with the *words we choose to believe* about ourselves. Words that were planted in our minds by friends, relatives, teachers and clergy, regarding what they thought we could or could not become as viewed through their own autobiographies. Words that would either inspire us to great accomplishments or deflate our ambitions before we took even the smallest step forward. We choose which words to hear and upon believing them to be true, set out to live—what will become—the story of our lives.

The other day, while standing in the checkout line at a local grocery store, I saw an angry young woman screaming at her *terrible two's* toddler. "Why can't you ever do anything right?" she said, as she proceeded to grab the child by the arm and drag him from the store. "Why can't you be more like your sister?" I wanted to run over to the little guy, hold him in my arms and tell him that mommy didn't really mean what she just said. My aching heart wanted to offer words of love and kindness—perhaps healing the wounds that had just been inflicted on this beautiful child. But instead, I bit down hard on my lower lip and said a small prayer.

Moments later, as I walked to my car, I could hear more of the same language—more of the same ugly words—as the women hastily threw her groceries in the trunk and drove away. What will that child become? I wondered. What chance does he have, at such a young and tender age, to overcome words so carelessly delivered, so innocently received?

Of course children are not the only ones who fall victim to the reckless and controlling use of words by others. Verbal abuse is an enormous problem in our society, particularly within the confines of a marriage. Often, it is the dominating ego of one of the partners that sets the tone for what the other can do, say or even believe.

I once knew a couple where the husband was always the controlling factor. In everything they did, it was *his way or the highway*. He frequently abused her verbally in public, talking down to her with harsh words of criticism and insults, all the while keeping her in her place and focused on his needs and desires. Ranting and raving about everything under the sun, he *never allowed her to have an original opinion*, thought or even a friendship without his approval. To this day, she has yet to blossom into the person she was meant to be. His words have kept her locked up in shackles and chains.

But it isn't only the words of others that define our direction in life; it's also the words we speak to ourselves. What we hear in our heads—that small little voice—is often more powerful and controlling than anything anyone else could ever say to us. The good news, however, is that just as we have a choice regarding whether or not we listen to the words of others, we also *have a choice* as to what we tell ourselves about ourselves.

French pharmacist Emile Cou'e, quite by accident, discovered the placebo effect. Working late one night, he was approached by a man with severe abdominal pain requesting a drug for which he had no prescription. Wanting to help but not wanting to break the law, Emile told the man he was out of that particular drug and suggested a substitute that would work just as well. The man took Emile's advice and within days reported that he had been cured of his stomach problems. The substitute drug Emile had prescribed? Sugar.

Having witnessed first hand the *power of suggestion*, Emile thought that it might be possible to cure minor personality disorders by changing self-talk—the words we tell ourselves about ourselves—to more positive affirmations. Emile asked people diagnosed with low self esteem, to repeat the words "Every day, in every way, I'm getting better and better" at least twenty times a day for two months. The results were nothing less than astounding! Once negative and depressed, these folks were now facing life with an improved mental attitude. The shroud of darkness that had fallen over their lives had been lifted. Words—not drugs—were the cure.

Jesus, like other spiritual masters, understood the power of words and the lasting effect they could have on our lives and the lives of others. *"But I say to you that for every idle word men may speak, they will give account of it in the day of judgment. For by your words you will be justified and by your words you will be condemned"*—Matthew 12:36

Is it possible that the words we speak in this life will define us for all of eternity? Certainly worth considering before we open our mouths to speak…

Words are powerful tools; the very building blocks of our existence. Used with love and kindness, words can convey a sense of possibility and hope, comfort and encouragement. Words can build lasting friendships, mend torn relationships and bridge the vast differences between cultures and beliefs. Words can be one of the greatest gifts we can ever give to ourselves or another human being. Wrap them in bright colors, tie them with a bow and always, always, choose them wisely.

Some Things To Consider

Pick a day this week and consciously notice the words you say to others. And just as importantly—perhaps, more importantly—notice the words you say to yourself about yourself. Are they words of love and encouragement or words of fear and defeat? Change your inner and outer dialog and become an inspiration to others and to yourself.

BECOME YOUR HIGHEST GIFT

"A musician must make music, an artist must paint, a poet must write, if he is to be ultimately at peace with himself."

Abraham Maslow

Jesus could have played it safe and remained a carpenter His entire life. After all, it was a profession He knew well, and something that would have paid the bills and kept a roof over His head. By choosing the life of a carpenter, He could have avoided all together, the trials and pain He suffered during His short life. But thankfully, Jesus knew His true calling; His highest gift. He left the hammers and nails to someone else while He focused on the fire that burned in His heart—the mission He knew He must carry out.

Many successful people, in all walks of life, started out as something else before realizing what it is they were put on earth to do. I am often fascinated by the autobiographies of famous people and how at early stages of their lives they found themselves heading off in a direction that would lead them miles away from their true calling; their highest gift. Eventually, however, they found their way home and became the people God meant for them to be.

My wife Jan is a wonderful example. For eighteen years we put the idea of having children on the back burner while we both grew our careers and chased financial success. A little over four years ago we decided to try and have a baby. Or, should I say, Jan *knew in her heart* it was time and lovingly convinced me it was something we should do.

As we both turned forty, our beautiful son Josh was born and Jan became a mother for the first time. Seeing her today, as she cheerfully goes about the duties of motherhood, you know that being a mom is one of the things her soul came to earth to do. Yes, the world can rest a little safer knowing that another child is being nurtured and loved by a kind and caring soul. Jan has become one of her highest gifts—a mom!

What is the truth that lives in your heart? What is your highest gift? For many of us, what we do to make a living has nothing to do with where our passion lies. Somehow, perhaps because of the wishes of our parents or the limitations we placed on ourselves, we have chosen a lesser gift, or worse yet; become something that we are not. We live *unauthentic lives* and while this certainly affects our well-being as individuals, it also has a negative impact on the world as a whole.

I have often wondered how much better the world would be if everyone who loved to dance became a dancer. If every soul who could harness the creativity of a paintbrush, spent all of their waking hours creating beautiful pictures on canvass. Or those with the passion to sing allowed their voices to bring happiness to others. *What if everyone practiced their highest gift and did the very thing they knew they should be doing* instead of compromising and settling for something less, something safe.

Some will argue that *they do not know* what their highest gift is. To that I would say, *listen to your heart and follow your intuition*. In most cases, your highest gift is something that *comes naturally and causes time to stand still* whenever you do it. Take whatever your gift may be, nurture it, grow it and let it expand. Don't be afraid to fail or make mistakes. Don't be afraid to venture out of your comfort zone. Take baby-steps toward your true calling and start part-time while you continue to earn a living at your current job. Do whatever you need to do to take that first step forward—but take it!

A couple of years after our son was born, Jan decided to take a pottery class. Early in her life, back around the age of sixteen, she had discovered her artistic abilities. She even went so far as to begin college as an art major. But like many would-be artists, following her bliss and moving towards her desires seemed a little too risky and *far too impractical* for the "real world." So, for almost twenty-five years she kept the artist-within neatly hidden away.

Almost from the moment she began the class, her talent began to soar! The passion she had kept buried inside for so long was finally being released and her soul loved every minute of it! Today, she has built a studio in our home and is busy making the world a more beautiful place as her hands *turn the earth to art*. It all began with one little pottery class—one little *baby-step* towards the truth that lived in her soul.

Much of the stress we experience in life, and much of the stress we create for others, is caused from the imbalance we experience by being someone or something we are not. We find it difficult to love others and really contribute to the world, because we haven't yet figured out how to *love the one we're with*—ourselves. We may fool ourselves and even the world for a while—perhaps making a good living while doing it—but deep inside where it really counts, we are miserable, out of synch, and dying a slow death each and every day. In such a state, is it any wonder happiness alludes us?

One of my favorite movies is "Dead Poets Society." In one of the scenes, the teacher, played by Robin Williams, shows his students an old picture of a graduating class from many decades prior. In so many words, he explains to the class that while all of the people in the picture had their own hopes, their own dreams and their own gifts, all are now deceased and pushing up tulips in cemeteries. "You only get one chance to make a difference in this world," he continues. "Carpe diem! Seize the day!"

We serve no useful purpose by going through life, biding our time, while ignoring our highest gift—what it is we know we should be doing—our role in the universe. Our time on earth is but equal to the space between two words in a paragraph. Sooner than we think, the last grain of sand will have made its way from the top to the bottom of the hourglass. The decisions we placed on our "to do" list—planning to get to *someday*—will no longer be available to us. Another generation will have replaced us. Our time on earth will be over.

The world is waiting to hear the unique song God placed in your heart. You are the only one who can play the notes, for you are the only one who knows what they are. Somewhere in the depths of your soul, lying dormant, just waiting to be found, is your highest gift—the instrument God gave you to play. Dust it off, tune it up and let the music begin!

Some Things To Consider

Are you currently doing what you came to earth to do? Do you look forward to the start of each new day and the opportunity it brings for you to seize the moment? Is there a nagging in your heart that says the way life *turned out* is not the way it should be? If you're not living your highest gift, someone else is *picking up the slack* and doing your part. Maybe its time for you to take off the mask of the person people want you to be and become the person that you are.

ONE CLEAR VOICE

"God still speaks to those who take the time to listen."
Unknown

From dawn till dusk we chase our elusive desires. Forever reaching, forever striving, we grasp for that which is just beyond our reach. In the continuing search for something better—a pasture greener or a moment more splendid—we sacrifice the present and lose sight of our soul. Our lives become a constant craving for that which we do not have. Materialistic desires over-rule our spiritual needs as the power of gold mesmerizes us and dollar signs perform their seductive dance in our heads. Money becomes something that must be sought after, saved and protected. The frantic pace takes our breath away and reduces us to rats in a race against time.

The daily pressures of life can often consume our present moments. We load our minds with instant replays of past mistakes or futuristic thoughts of how much better life will be when we finally arrive, finally get what it is we want, finally become what we are not. Our hearts scream in defiance, but we do not listen. We push onward towards a victory in someone else's race and follow a road map of success designed by someone other than ourselves. If we make it to the finish line, we find that it is often littered with ladders of success placed against the wrong wall.

We are often confused by the daily static that somehow invades our minds. Our attention is drawn away from the important, only to focus on the urgent. Some of us feel misled, for we have known the important—our own personal truth—as it beckoned us to its doorstep with promises of balance and love, kindness and grace. It offered us redemption and a chance to recapture the souls we may have somehow lost.

Whenever we have slowed our raging minds long enough to notice, we have caught a glimpse of this beauty—truly heaven on earth. Through meditation and prayer we have seen how wonderful life can be through the eyes of an innocent child. Where only the *now* exists and life is non-judgmental and pure, rather than false, phony and obscene.

Life often gives the impression that making it through another day is all that matters. That striving—but never arriving—is what it's all about. For many of us, never does the sun set that we do not think about tomorrow at the expense of today. What needs to be done? What mountains need to be conquered? In doing so, we sacrifice the only thing we really own—the moment at hand.

Then, just when we begin to feel as if tomorrow is most important, our minds flash back to what happened yesterday. We remember and dwell upon the mistakes we made—how things coulda-shoulda-woulda been different if only we would have taken a different course—had a better plan. Rather than releasing the past and all of our mistakes, we relive the pain over and over again, unable to offer forgiveness to the people who need it most—ourselves.

Our hearts race and our minds leap ahead until conclusions are drawn—right or wrong—about what the future may hold. We worry. We are consumed with guilt. We dwell endlessly on the things that we have done and things that we have failed to do, until all of this noise in our heads drowns out the voice that is calling to us, begging us to listen.

But I know of a powerful silence, a tranquil oasis that lives within reach of all of us. I go there often to seek solace and serenity and peace—to replenish life from within. But mostly, I go there to listen for God's voice. For I have found that in moments of solitude and total retreat, He will speak to me. Amidst the confusion and total chaos of a world gone seem-ingly mad, *one clear voice* can be heard. A voice that calms my impatience, leads me to peaceful meadows and holds the promise for acceptance of the world just as it is. I cup my hands and drink from these living waters. My thirst is quenched; my soul reborn.

I frequent this meditative state whenever the ways of the world become unbearable. Whenever I need to remind myself of the reason I am here—my life's purpose and mission—and that all is not wrong in the world. I go there to listen. To openly and honestly tune into the one clear voice that tells me everything will be OK. The voice that speaks to my heart in a language the mind cannot understand. The voice that assures me I am one with the universe. I go there to commune with God—I have never been disappointed.

With all that seems evil in our world, with all the madness that permeates our lives, take time to be quiet and still; to meditate and pray. Connect to the God Force and realize your life's purpose. Embrace the gifts He has given you and set out to be the person you see in those quiet times.

For in those moments of spiritual connection, God will communicate the role you can play in making the world a better place. He will quiet the yearning in your heart, offer contentment and peace, and allow you to rest in the supportive arms of spirit. The real you, the one that has been pacing the cage all these years, will be set free. You will find your bliss in the garden of silence.

The voice is there to gently speak to all of us. It knows no particular language, nor does it identify with race, status, culture or religion. It is available at any moment we choose no matter where we are, no matter who we are. But to hear it, we must quiet our minds, pay attention and really listen. Do it. Go there. Enter this peaceful dimension between nowhere and now here and change your life forever.

Some Things To Consider

Take some time today and quiet your mind. Find a peaceful place to relax and just listen to the silence. If you've never meditated before, don't worry about doing anything special. Just close your eyes, breathe in deeply and slowly exhale. You don't have to sit in a funny position or chant any-thing in particular unless you choose to. As thoughts come into and out of your mind, acknowledge them and let them go. Enjoy!

Choose To Be Happy

*"People are just about as happy
as they make up their minds to be."*
Abraham Lincoln

Happiness is a choice. Whether we see the glass as half full or half empty, so it will be and so it will further become. The bridge that connects the happiness we seek with the reality we experience, is constructed by our ability to pause in the gap between stimulus and response and *choose love over fear*. We must rest in the knowledge that we are perfect in the eyes of God, just the way we are. We must commit to living our truth, manifesting our destiny and *allowing happiness* to permeate our entire being. Life was never meant to be a struggle. There is nothing to be fearful of.

Yet, many of us are afraid to be happy. It's almost as if we believe that if everything is going well something bad must surely be around the next corner. We want so desperately to feel at peace and *one with the universe*, yet, we refuse to allow the light of happiness to illuminate our lives. Feeling good often makes us feel guilty. How can I be so happy when so much is wrong in the world? we ask. Yet, how can we not be happy? Happiness is our birthright.

To escape the burden of negative thoughts, we must discard a scarcity mentality that suggests that *happiness is of limited supply* and embrace the belief that it's OK to be happy; that there is *plenty of happiness for everyone*. We must come to understand that our being happy will not result in others being miserable. That our success will not result in others failing. That our peace and happiness will not result in pain and sorrow for others. We must surrender to the notion that *happiness is not like a pie with only so many pieces to go around*—happiness is abundantly available. We need only make the choice to partake of it.

I know, I know—life is full of problems. We just finish dealing with one issue and another dilemma comes along which seems twice as bad as the crisis we faced last week. There is a saying within Alcoholics Anonymous that "Every problem comes bearing it's own solution." God provides the answer to every problem the moment it occurs. But we just can't see that. Instead, we focus our attention on all that is wrong and carry our pain as if it was *our cross to bear.* Happiness eludes us because *we become absorbed in the problem, blinded to the solution.* Our lack of positive thinking prevents us from seeing what could be.

Many years ago, I read a book by the late Norman Vincent Peale titled "Positive Imaging." The concept of the book is based on the belief that if you *vividly picture in your mind a desired state of happiness and hold that image until it sinks into your unconscious mind*, great, untapped energies will be released and your goal will be realized. The technique works best when combined with a deep spiritual faith *backed by prayer and meditation* as well as the seemingly illogical practice of giving thanks for benefits before they are received. By expecting good things to happen you force all negative thoughts from your consciousness and allow the universe to manifest your desires. It has worked wonders in my own life.

I can hear many of you say, "But if I pretend that everything is going right and expect only good things to happen, I'm not being truly honest with myself." But why should we believe that *negative thoughts are any more "honest" than positive ones?* How is it that we have come to resist positive thoughts and focus instead on only that which is negative? Are we more comfortable hiding our spirit behind a wall of darkness as opposed to letting our light shine?

By letting our light shine and ignoring the urge to be negative, we let optimism prevail and become a beacon of hope and possibility in the lives of others. Positive thoughts are powerful thoughts—thoughts that can change the world. Positive thoughts are thoughts of love. Perhaps that's why we're so afraid of them.

The little voice in our heads often says, "Don't set your sights too high. You might be disappointed." But setting our sights high, chasing our dreams and focusing on all that will make the world a better place, is exactly what we should be doing. It is the feeling of guilt that, perhaps, we don't deserve to have what we desire—that somehow we are not worthy of happiness—that holds us back. But to be truly happy, we must push every bit of negative thinking from our minds and focus instead on positive affirmations. Negative thoughts will continue to raise their ugly heads but when they do, we should acknowledge their existence and then release them from our consciousness—forever!

Once we set fear aside, embrace love and set our sights on pure and noble pursuits, it is perhaps equally important to fully engage in the process of *doing*. The people who   seem most happy in life are "doers." They're involved in the process of living and contributing to a better world each and everyday. They have little time for complainers and those who set on the sidelines or play Monday morning quarterback. They are *in the arena* making their dreams come true. Regrets? They have a few. But as the song says, "Too few to mention."

To choose happiness, we must *relinquish the need to be right*. When we allow ourselves to get caught up in the madness of defending our position—whatever the subject may be—we trade happiness for the privilege of falling on our own swords. Taking our opinions and ourselves too seriously can result in discontent and a feeling that we are *separate from* and not connected to those around us. Our ego wants us to believe that we are somehow better than everyone else.

But, self-imposed superiority—the belief that we are somehow better than others—is a fear driven, sure-fire way to be unhappy. It is a choice that *creates barriers* and pushes us further and further away from the love and support of those around us. Conversely, by allowing ourselves to *feel connected spiritually to everyone* on the planet, we cease to judge others as either better or worse than ourselves. We become more open to acceptance and understanding. The world becomes less black and white and a little more gray. In this state of oneness with the universe, happiness presents itself as a strand of yarn that weaves through our collective souls and binds us together with an unseen power. We begin to see the eyes of our brothers and sisters in the face of every human being.

Sadly, whether in a court of law or over coffee, it has become almost fashionable these days to *blame our unhappiness* on the actions of others. Yet, in truth— in and of themselves—the actions of others cannot cause us any pain. They are simply actions. We *choose* how to respond to the actions of others and *in our choosing*, are either illuminated in the light of happiness or swallowed by the darkness of anger and hatred.

The actions of others have *absolutely no control over our happiness* other than the control we *choose* to give them. By acknowledging that happiness lies within our control, we place the decision of being happy on ourselves and begin to become more aware of the power that lies within us. We take responsibility for own happiness. We rise to the occasion and begin to take charge of our lives.

Perhaps the *most important tool* in our decision to be happy, is the ability to forgive. The wings of forgiveness can often take us to heights we never dreamed we could achieve. Forgiveness eliminates the *head noise* and internal dissonance that can cloud our judgment and blind us from seeing the happiness around us. By *forgiving others* as well as ourselves, we surrender to the power of innocence and grace. We allow peace to surround our souls. We *drain the poison of hate and anger* from our veins. We no longer have any attachment to the outcome but focus only on the moment at hand. Forgiveness frees us to be happy.

A few years ago, while meditating one Sunday morning, it became clear that my inner peace was being stifled by the anger and resentment I still harbored for another human being—a once-upon-a-time friend and the builder of my home. Two years had passed and I was still *blaming him* for problems we incurred during construction. I was still blaming him for *my pain*. At that moment, I felt God urging me to pick up the phone and call him. I was perplexed—I had no idea what I was going to say!

I made the uncomfortable phone call later that evening and found, to my surprise, words of love and forgiveness rolling from my tongue. I had no attachment to the outcome, no need for reconciliation—only the need to give unconditional love; expecting nothing in return. As I hung up the phone, a blissful feeling rushed through my body. For two years I had put off saying what needed to be said. I knew we probably would never be friends again but now through the power of forgiveness, I could move on with my life. My wounds had been healed. Happiness prevailed.

From Moby Dick, Herman Melville writes: "For as this appalling ocean surrounds the verdant land, so in the soul of man there lies one insular Tahiti, full of peace and joy, but encompassed by all the horrors of the half-lived life." Can you imagine the pain and sorrow we would each feel having reached the end of our lives knowing there was so much more we could have done, so much more we could have been?

In our *pursuit of happiness*, we must listen to and understand the message that is written in our hearts and do what it tells us to do—no exceptions. We must live our lives with purpose and courage. We must follow our bliss even if the path we choose runs counter to the opinions of others—true happiness is not decided by committee. We must do whatever God put us on earth to do with *passion and determination*, knowing we only have a short time in which to do it. Anything less will result in a half-lived life; a life devoid of purpose, mission and ultimately happiness. Don't let it happen to you…

We are at the beginning of another year; a new millennium. Over the next twelve months we will each be given another 365 days during which we may choose happiness or sorrow. We can rise each morning full of exuberance and excitement, ready to take on the day or we can curse the rising of the sun; shunning its warmth and closing our eyes to its brightness. We can welcome each new day with the declaration: "Good morning God!" or "Good god—morning!" The choice is ours to make.

Some Things To Consider

Are you choosing to be happy? List five things you've done in the past month to bring happiness into your life.

Who do you need to forgive? Why haven't you done so? List the people, including yourself if appropriate, that need your forgiveness. Write a letter of forgiveness to each of them and then follow up with a phone call.

LET YOUR COMPASS BE YOUR GUIDE

"We don't have to agree on an exact route or head down the same road, we just have to trust our inner spiritual direction and walk towards the love that lives in our hearts. In the end, we will all arrive safe and sound at the same destination—the same God—though we may not have traveled the same path in getting there."

Jeffrey Alan Hall

"Forget the map," Jim declared. "The *compass* is the only thing that will get us out of here alive!"

Springtime in the Rockies, and there we were: two experienced hikers wandering around in circles, somewhere in the San Juan mountain range. In the thick of the forest, our map had offered little help as we pushed our way through blinding snow and howling winds. I began to worry as late afternoon turned to darkness. We were wet. We were cold. We were lost.

The *compass* turned out to be the best little piece of gear we had packed that day. By using it to consistently monitor our direction, we were able to arrive safely back at our car just as our nose hairs began to freeze. A Thermos full of Starbuck's finest steamed up the windows as we *romanced the bean* and gave thanks for our safe return. The *compass* had saved our lives…

Losing our way spiritually can seem just as frightening. As *darkness of the soul* sets in, we frantically look for a map that will lead us towards the light. Trouble is, there are so many different maps, so many different beliefs. How do we know which one to choose? And, do we really have to choose? Or is there, perhaps, another way to connect to Spirit—a way that needs no map but, rather, relies only on our own inner sense of direction?

Can we trust our own *spiritual compass* to guide us through the dark or will *the boogieman get us* if we don't watch out?

Like spokes in a wheel, we are all connected to God at the center. But, also like spokes in a wheel, we come to the center (God) from different directions. Some of us arrive as Christians or Buddhists, as Jews or Muslims, as Taoists or Hindus and everything in between. Others connect through what has been labeled the *New Age* movement or through their own unique spiritual path. Just as a compass points north no matter where we are, so too will our spiritual compass point to God no matter what our religion or faith. *It makes no difference how we connect to Spirit, only that we do.*

A map only works if you *already know where you're starting from.* Spiritually speaking, most of us have little or no idea where we're starting from; we only know where we want to go—towards God. That's what's so great about a compass: We don't have to agree on an exact route or head down the same road, we just have to trust our inner spiritual direction and walk towards the love that lives in our hearts. In the end, *we will all arrive safe and sound at the same destination—the same God—though we may not have traveled the same path in getting there.*

Beginning as early as pre-school, we are taught that there is *only one correct answer* to a test question. Everything becomes a dichotomy—yes or no, right or wrong, true or false, black or white. We get *programmed* early to think in terms of absolutes and, sadly, we come to ignore the wondrous possibilities that lie in the gray areas of life—or as I like to call it—*life between the piano keys*, where synchronicity and creativity rule.

But here's the good news: Along the path of light we don't have to play the silly games we learned in school. Because in the world of Spirit, there is no right or wrong, no cheat sheet, *no absolute truth.* Sure, you can still sneak a peek over the shoulder of someone else when you think no one's looking, but it won't do you any good. Why? Because how we choose to connect to God can be as unique and individual as we are. There is no true or false, no multiple choice. Finding our way spiritually is an essay question of the highest degree where *each of us is awarded a passing grade*. As long as love is what guides us, there can be *no* wrong answers.

It helps to understand that since the same God that created the universe created us, we can *surrender to this infinite power and trust It to lead us* through the darkness and into the light. Nothing special is required to connect to this power—we just need to go inside ourselves and listen. You see, God didn't stop speaking to us 2,000 years ago, and He or She or It—or whatever else you choose to call the God Force—doesn't speak to just a few privileged people today. God speaks to each of us directly and honestly with unconditional love.

To hear God, you don't have to conform to some impossible standard or learn a secret code. You don't have to cram into the same phone booth as everyone else, place a collect call and hope that God will accept the charges. Nope. God set it up so we could converse with Him any time and anywhere. There's no charge. Not even for *roaming!* We just have to quiet our minds and stop talking long enough to hear Him.

For some of us, hitching our wagon to the organized beliefs of a church, synagogue or mosque is the right path to take. For others, *a map* drawn by the autobiography of a charismatic leader will take them to the spiritual oasis they seek. But, sometimes those choices can lead to a major roadblock, where rules and rituals keep *the experience of God* at arms length—just out of reach—the equivalent of standing knee deep in a river and dying of thirst. The spiritual connection gets *short-circuited* because structure and rules only get in the way of a *one-on-one relationship* with the Creator. Remember: There is you and there is God. Nothing else is required. Nothing.

When your thirst for a connection to God becomes insatiable—when it seems that you are *spiritually lost* and the answers you're getting *just don't seem to fit*—seek guidance from your *internal compass* and listen to your heart. Spend some quiet time in meditation and prayer. Read from the Bible, the Koran, *A Course In Miracles* or whatever other spiritual literature appeals to you. Take a hike. Buy a puppy. But then *stop*—let it all sink in. How does it feel? Just right or one size too small? Need to suck in your gut just to get the zipper up? Or, does it feel comfortable and relaxed like a pair of your favorite jeans.

Compare what you have read and heard—what everyone else says you *should* believe— with the *truth that lives in your soul*. Graciously accept the various maps of those who wish to *show you the way*. Digest their knowledge and truth with love and compassion. Wish them well along *their chosen path* and make plans to meet up with them somewhere in the afterlife if you wish.

Then, when no one is looking, *burn all the maps!* Let your internal compass be your guide. Go with your feelings and head off in the direction that seems right—*for you.* You won't be alone—there's a whole bunch of us out here *dancing barefoot in the rain.* And you know what else? God's here too!

Some Things To Consider

Does your relationship to God seem right for you? Do you know God or just believe in God? Are you following a map or your own compass? Do you hear God speaking to you personally or do you rely on the autobiographies and the experiences of others? Have you ever been so happy that you danced barefoot in the rain?

I DARE YOU!

"Stand boldly on the precipice of life and fear not what lie ahead. Stretch out your arms and embrace the lady of chance. Walk the tight rope without a net—out on the fringes where all the action is. Inhale a deep and intoxicating breath of courage and take a leap of faith. Conquer the fear within, set sail in uncharted waters, and ride on the winds of bliss. Move away from what seems safe and towards what feels right. Become your highest gift. I dare you!"

Jeffrey Alan Hall

There we were—six of us—legends in our own minds—perched high on the edge of a jagged cliff some forty-feet above the raging river below. Looking up from the ground, it had all seemed so simple—a cakewalk—climb up the side of the rock and dive fearlessly into the water. But now, after an exhausting trek up a wet and slippery trail in forty-five degree weather, I wasn't so sure. I stood there facing a very big *first step*—cold, shivering and scared out of my mind!

A bunch of college freshmen, we had taken the summer off to volunteer as park rangers in Yellowstone. We thought of ourselves as macho, thrill seeking, mountain-men, hell bent on taming the West. But as we peeked over the edge of what seemed like Mount Everest, I didn't exactly feel *like John Wayne*. Truth be told, I wondered how in the heck I got into this mess! Was there any way a respectable, *self-proclaimed mountain man* could, maybe, sneak back down to the safety below without anyone noticing? I had no sooner considered my *escape route* when suddenly words that sent testosterone shooting through my veins filled the air.

"We dare you!"

Our girlfriends had taken on the role of cheerleaders and were now *challenging our masculinity* from the comfortable safety of lawn chairs scattered along the shore. Those *three little words* summoned all of our collective courage. Call it stupidity, a total lack of respect for our own mortality or simply *wanting to impress the girls*, but suddenly each of us jumped as if our manhood were at stake. We hit the river feet first with a force that turned the water into concrete—surfaced—and grinning from ear to ear, slapped high-fives. We had conquered our fears and most importantly, we had survived. We almost drown from laughing so hard!

What about you? Are you standing on the edge of your own *self-made* cliff afraid to move forward and jump into the waters of life? Do you need someone to simply say, "I dare you?" If you feel this way, you're not alone. A recent Harris poll found that 65% of baby-boomers are dissatisfied with their lives. Many of us feel that we have yet to realize our dreams and reach our full potential. Many of us feel trapped and afraid to change. We stand on the precipice looking towards a better tomorrow, but we just can't seem to find the courage to jump.

But what are we so afraid of? Why do we think we must *tip toe* from womb to tomb? What do we think we will lose?—our lives? If we are afraid to live for fear of dying, doesn't that make us dead already? If we can't live the life we truly desire, what's the point of living?

If you see yourself in this scenario and you're ready to make some serious changes in your life, *I dare you* to take a minute and read the challenges I've listed below. They're not easy to implement and each will take some time to get use to. But if you're really serious about becoming the person you were meant to be, you have to begin to think differently about life. The definition of insanity is to *do things the way you've always done them but expect a different outcome*. Don't fall for that trap. Vow to change your life right here, right now.

I dare you to...

- Live the unimaginable life, a life built upon *your* dreams, hopes and desires. Don't wait to see it *before* you believe it. Believe it and you *will* see it! Act upon your own definition of what it means to be truly alive and *never settle* for anything less. Decide what your legacy will be and begin to live it!

- Listen deeply to your hearts desire and believe in the *one clear voice* that resides within your soul and knows you better than any other human being ever could. Go *within* to find the answers. Be still and embrace the silence. Become comfortable with only yourself, your thoughts, your being. Know that you are complete and *perfect* just as you are.

- Learn to manifest your own destiny. You *can* control and determine the course your life will take. The same power that flows through the Universe flows through you. Harness the power within. Jesus said, "Ye too will be gods." Believe it! Act upon it!

- Volunteer for *anything* that involves extending a helping hand to another. Get up and out of your comfort zone and throw yourself into a cause—any cause—that will improve mankind. Become an angel for someone—anyone—that needs your special gifts. Encourage another human being to *reach for the stars* and be the best they can be. Coach them to their highest potential and be there when they need a friend.

- Love with unbridled passion and truly *commit yourself to another* without fear of rejection or in an attempt to get something in return. Just give—give until it hurts. Your pain will be replaced by an abundance of love as it flows back to you, often from sources you never knew existed.

- Listen for the *cliquing noise*—that unmistakable sound of compromise and *follow the herd* mentality. Walk away from *any* group or organization (religious or otherwise) that *expects* you to behave in a certain way. If it feels like a clique, it *is* a clique. God did not intend for us to behave like cattle. Can I hear an "Amen!"

- Vow to *eliminate all toxic relationships* from your life once and for all. Life is too short to put up with anyone who abuses you physically, mentally or spiritually. Surround yourself with *only those* who will offer a helping hand along the path of light. Look for cheerleaders not nay-sayers. Choose your friends carefully. Hang out with only those people that *walk the talk*. Do their actions match up with their beliefs? If not, move on. Phony people are a dime a dozen.

- Live simply, yet comfortably. Ignore the advertising campaigns of Madison Avenue and purchase only those things you *truly need*. Try putting a week or two between your desire for something and actually purchasing it. If you do this you will be surprised how many things simply *fade away from your desires*. Live within your means. Spend less than your weekly paycheck and save the unspent portion. Life is easier to navigate with money in the bank. When you don't need a job to survive from week to week, decisions about your future become easier to make.

- Worry less about how you look and more about how you think. Spend as much time exercising your mind as you do your body. Strive to *put plastic surgeons out of business* by becoming comfortable with your appearance. Let your inner light outshine any physical flaw that *you think* you may have. Wear the orange shirt with the purple plaid slacks if that feels like the right thing to do.

- Learn to have fun! When asked *what they would have done differently* if they could live their lives over, a group of centurions replied, "Eat more ice cream!" Enjoy each moment as if it were your last. (And don't forget the chocolate sprinkles on top!)

We were all put on earth to live authentic lives—it's our *absolute* birthright. Yet sadly, many of us will come to the end of our lives having *lived someone else's dream*—spending far too much of our precious time working at jobs and living lives that should have belonged to someone else. Our work life and our personal life (often intertwined) must be in alignment with our highest ideals and beliefs or we will dread every minute of every day. Believing in world peace but working in a bomb factory *because you need the money* will not make for a happy camper.

But, then, maybe you don't work in a bomb factory but don't work at something you *really love* either. Maybe you never really *showed up* for your life but, rather, let life kind of *happen to you*. Perhaps you got so swept up in the raging waters of *just trying to earn a living* that now reversing or even modifying your direction seems all but impossible. But guess what, it doesn't have to be that way. You *can be* the person you were meant to be. You *can* live a genuine and uniquely different life—the life that is *you and no one else*.

How? Stand boldly on the precipice of life and fear not what lie ahead. Stretch out your arms and embrace the lady of chance. Walk the tight rope without a net—out on the fringes where all the action is. Inhale a deep and intoxicating breath of courage and take a leap of faith. Conquer the fear within, set sail in uncharted waters, and ride on the winds of bliss. Move away from what seems safe and towards what feels right. Become your highest gift. And for crying out loud, eat more ice cream! I dare you!

Some Things To Consider

What does *your* cliff look like? Why are you afraid to jump off? Who's watching you? Who will dare you? Find that person—the one who can get you to jump—and beg them to stand behind you and push!

WHERE THERE IS HATRED, LET ME SOW LOVE

"At certain moments, always unforeseen, I become happy....I look at strangers near as if I have known them all my life...everything fills me with affection...It may be an hour before the mood passes, but ultimately I seem to understand that I enter upon it the moment I cease to hate."

William Butler Yeats

There was once a very old and wise man who was enjoying the afternoon with his grandchildren when he posed the question: *How do you know the night is over and the day has come?* The children grew silent and pondered the question for several minutes.

Finally one of them spoke up, "You will know the night is over and the day has come when at dawn, you look out at a tree and you can tell whether it is an apple or a pear tree."

The old man politely acknowledged this response, but then repeated the question. This time, without pause, a second child stood up and said, "You will know the night is over and the day has come when you see an animal in the distance and you can tell whether it is a donkey or a horse." Again the old man politely acknowledged this response, but shaking his head, he repeated the question one more time.

The children, now too puzzled to answer, begged their grandfather to solve the dilemma he had created. Looking each child directly in the eyes, he wrapped his arms around them and said with a smile, "You will know the night is over and the day has come when you look into the eyes of *any human being*, and see there your brother or your sister. For *if you do not see your brother or your sister, it is still night—the day has yet to come.*"

In America, the face of our brother or sister may look nothing like our own. We are what we have always been—*a wonderful melting pot* of all human beings that inhabit the earth—a microcosm of the entire planet—a little of this and a little of that. We come in different colors and with different beliefs. Perhaps nowhere on earth is there more diversity of race and religion than right here in the good old USA. We are a diverse people and *our diversity is what makes us strong.*

Our respect for one another, our ability to set aside our differences and understand each other's truth, is precisely what our country was founded upon. *Brotherly-love* as it is sometimes called, has allowed different cultures to co-exist in this country for over two hundred years. It hasn't always been easy, especially in the area of racial tension, but we continue to *work at making it work.* As difficult as it is to live up to sometimes, most Americans seem to have a deep-down understanding—if not always visible— that *all men are created equal.* We feel a connection to each other that transcends our differences and allows us to live right next door to someone with different beliefs and yet still relate to them as Americans. I believe that *love* is what makes this all possible.

Love stands for what we are *for.* Hate stands for what we are *against.* Focusing on what we are *for* will always unite us, focusing on what we are *against* will only separate us and split us apart. Hate is demanding and asks. "What can I get?" Love makes no such demands and asks, "What can I give?" Hate is a physical solution that often seeks death and destruction. Love is a *spiritual solution* that always seeks peace and understanding. Hate harms. Love heals.

In his letters to the Corinthians, Saint Paul wrote, "Love never fails." The word *never* means *never.* It's pretty clear, right? Yet, in times of crisis and emotional despair, we often let our egos take over and attempt to seek solutions *not through love* but through hate—not through cooperation and understanding, but through *separation and intolerance.* Far too often we seek to be understood before we seek to understand. Because we are fearful, we go for the *quick fix* that hate often provides, afraid to *trust in the power of love.*

Whether we choose to wear turbans or baseball caps, whether our heads are shaved or covered by a Hijab, whether we worship in a church, a synagogue, a mosque or none of the above, we are all connected to the same body—the universal power of love. We must embrace this power and cast fear aside, for our fate—not just as a country— but also as a diverse global community, depends on this: Will we live our lives in fear or in love?

To answer that question, consider the world's religions. Listed below are paraphrases from various religious groups. Notice how every group can agree on one thing—love. Love— *not fear*—is the common denominator that links all religions together under a unified *spiritual* umbrella. No matter what our faith, we all seem to *share a common belief* in love.

Buddhism: Let a man cultivate toward the whole world a heart of love.

Christian: God is love and you are God's children of the most high.

Islam: Love is this, that thou shouldst account thyself very little and God very great.

Judaism: Thou shall love the Lord thy God with all thy heart and thy neighbor as thy self.

Sikhism: God will regenerate those in whose hands there is love.

Hinduism: One can best worship the Lord through love.

New Age: All spiritual paths lead to God and God is love.

A Course in Miracles teaches, " I can choose peace rather than this." In every grave hour—in the gap between stimulus and response—lies the *freedom to choose* love over hate. We always have the option to take a deep breath and pause just long enough to be responsible—response-able— able to respond. In doing so, we can *choose peace* and thus *create a world* built upon the solid rock of love as opposed to the shifting sands of hate.

Love is the universal light that illuminates the heart and soul of every human being on earth—all six billion of us. Love is the spiritual bridge that spans our religious and cultural differences and leads us towards the path of tolerance and understanding. It is the spiritual glue that holds the universe together. Love gives us the power to mend fences, offer forgiveness and embrace the future with courage and hope. It is always there when we need it and it truly *never fails*.

I *borrowed* the title of this essay from a wonderful prayer written by Saint Francis of Assisi. Saint Francis, the son of a rich merchant, felt *lost* most of his life until he had a vision of what his *life purpose* should be. The vision changed his life forever and from that moment forward he abstained from all falsehood and any thoughts of harming others. Instead, he focused his thoughts only on the power of love and how he could use that power to make the world a better place.

The words of Saint Francis were written during the thirteenth century but they are as relevant today as they were then. As you read these powerful words, consider how our lives, our country and our planet could benefit if each of us chose to live our lives in just this way.

> Lord, make me an instrument of thy peace.
> Where there is hatred, let me sow love;
> Where there is injury, pardon;
> Where there is doubt, faith;
> Where there is despair, hope;
> Where there is darkness, light;
> Where there is sadness, joy.
>
> O divine Master, grant that I may not so much seek
> To be consoled as to console,
> To be understood as to understand,
> To be loved as to love;
> For it is in giving that we receive;
> It is in pardoning that we are pardoned;
> It is in dying that we are born to eternal life.

Saint Francis Of Assisi

Let us sow love where once there was hate. Let us see our brothers and sisters in the eyes of every human being. Let us embrace tolerance and understanding. Let the night be over and the day begin.

Some Things To Consider

Get out a sheet of paper and list the times in your life when you used hate and anger to solve a problem. Now, on the same sheet of paper, make another list of when you used love to rectify a situation. Which list is longer? What were the differences in the outcome? How did you feel inside after it was over? Which solution—love or hate—was more long lasting?

PATHWAYS TO SURRENDER

"When you surrender, you remember that you are a Divine soul, inseparable from God, guided by God. You also see the absolute connection you have to all God's grace and good, like rays that are connected to the sun. What you see is your true worth as a child of the Universe, infinitely loved and supported."

Sonia Choquette

Would you like to experience heaven on earth? Would you like to get rid of all the unhappiness in your life and experience only joy? Does the idea of living a blissful existence, unencumbered by the weight of grief and sorrow appeal to you? Or, how about never having to worry about anything ever again? Does that sound good? Would you like a little of that?

You can have some you know—as much as you want. It's all within your reach and you don't need a prescription to get it. It's not illegal and it's absolutely 100% free! In fact, you already own your own personal stash—as much as you would like, anytime you're ready to use it. It's been with you since the beginning of time—since way back when—when your soul was *nowhere*—before it came to *now here*.

So, what do you have to do to get it? Nothing. In fact, thinking you have to *do* anything will only get in the way of receiving it. I know that sounds a little difficult to believe, but your *inability to believe* is precisely why you don't have it. There is nothing to chase, nothing to go after and nothing to search for. You don't need a translator, a guru, a building, a book, or someone *Holy* to show you the way. There is no map, no buried treasure, nothing to find. The only thing that's required is *surrender.*

Did it sound like I just swore at you? I mean did the word *surrender* just feel like a four letter word? Did it just make the hair on the back of your neck stand up? It can do that you know; this word *surrender*. Just the sound of it can make us feel like we lost something, gave up the fight or just plain quit trying. But in some ways that is exactly what you must do to find the peace I speak of—lose your ego, give up the fight and quit trying to find something that has already been given to you—already been found.

The fight, the chase, the endless pursuit, has only led you *down the path of fear*, further and further outside of yourself—further away from the truth. What you're looking for does not lie *out there* somewhere. What you're looking for lies within. That may be why it has eluded you all these years—you've been looking for it in all the wrong places.

You see many of us have been facing the wrong direction. We've been looking outward, away from ourselves, thinking that happiness is something we need to *find*. But, to find what we're looking for, we need only turn our eyes inward and begin to look where the answers really lie—*within the soul*.

It may be hard for you to believe, but the only reason you haven't experienced the happiness you desire—heaven on earth—is simply because you haven't chosen to—yet. You see, the God force allows you to choose your reality based on the lessons your soul came to earth to learn. The Universe trusts you to know what you want. It will accommodate *any request* as soon as you make it abundantly clear what your request is.

The God force doesn't make any judgment about what will or will not make you happy. It knows that what constitutes happiness will be different for everyone. It simply goes about its business, flowing through your life like a steady trade wind, until *you* make the choice to set your sails and flow with it. The secret isn't to find a way to change the direction of the Universe to fit your needs, the secret is to just relax and surrender to its power. The power of the God force will take you wherever you desire to go. It's always present and it's always free. The journey begins with the *choice* to surrender.

I know this can make you feel a little cheated, like someone has played a dirty trick on you all this time. After all, if you're like a lot of us, you probably bought into the religious notion that you were born in sin and thus needed to be forgiven before you could be deserving of happiness. You may have been led to believe that you had to do something, or become something or receive something or give $omething before the bearded old man who roams the sky would grant you a favor and toss down a few crumbs of joy.

But I don't believe you were born in sin, I believe you were born in love. I don't believe that God is some kind of judgmental angry old man who roams the sky; in fact, I don't believe that God is separate from us at all. I believe that God lives in us—each and every one of us. He is separate and apart from nothing. God is everything and thus, we are everything. We all have His power within us, but only a few of us have chosen to surrender to it. Some of us are still waiting to embrace our own truth.

If that's you, take a cleansing breath and send yourself some love. You see, a lot of us as children bought into the established views of religion and never questioned whether they were right for us. We just practiced our faith like everyone else in our family and never gave a whole lot of thought to what we were actually doing. But guess what? You can come out of the closet now. You don't have buy into it any longer unless you choose to; unless your religious practice is leading you to the spiritual place you desire. If it is, by all means continue along that path.

But for a lot of us, it's time to look in a different direction and consider that perhaps *God doesn't have a religion*. And maybe, just maybe, He doesn't have a beard. It might even be possible—heaven forbid— that He may not be a *He* after all. What if God is a She? What if God is neither? You can choose to see the God force anyway you wish if the way you currently see It doesn't feel right to you. My rule of thumb? If it makes me feel closer to God I accept it. If it tends to increase the separation between us, I run as fast as I can away from it!

That's why you will hear me use the term *God force* so often. For me, those two words seem to best describe the power that runs through my life, far better than any other option. Your choice may be much different than mine. A female client of mine once explained that she was unable to see God as a father figure because her own father had raped her repeatedly as a young girl. She was healing from a very traumatic childhood experience. By seeing God as a She, a roadblock was removed in her relationship to God that could have kept her feeling like an island—distant and removed.

By letting go and getting rid of anything that has kept you *separate from God* all this time, you can begin to consider the notion that perhaps you and God are not separate at all; that you and God might just be one and the same. Perhaps by seeing God in this new light and embracing our own *godliness*, we can allow more of God's energy—the power of love— to flow from us and into the world. Don't you think it just might be possible that God has heard all of our prayers for a better world—for a Savior—and He's already sent help? He's already sent you? Maybe it's time we let our own light shine, embrace our highest gifts and use them to make the planet a better place for everyone. Besides, doesn't just sitting around waiting to *be delivered* seem like a sorry substitution for the one-on-one relationship with God that you desire?

Take a good look inside yourself and tell me if what I am saying doesn't have just a little ring of truth to it. Don't you feel some inner sense of connection to everything in the universe? Haven't you always kind of felt that way? Doesn't it seem that if God created everything—and that includes you—that we could just relax, surrender to this awesome power and trust it to lead us to happiness? Doesn't it seem like it should be just that easy? Why would we ever think that connecting to God should be a struggle or that happiness requires a sacrifice? Do you really think God would have to play that kind of game? After all, He's God; He doesn't have to play any games. And since He is within us, neither do we.

Let me ask you something: Do you have to *make* a tulip grow? I don't mean plant the seed and do a little watering. I mean do you actually have to assist the seed in germinating, putting down roots, rising up from the soil and turning itself into a beautiful flower? And do you ever worry, as winter departs and spring arrives, that this could be the year it might not happen? That perhaps the tulips will forever cease to bloom? Of course not. You trust in Mother Nature—an unseen power greater than ourselves—and know that you don't have to worry about such things.

Or how about making the blood flow through your veins? Just before you fall asleep at night, do you worry that without your conscious help and involvement your heart might just stop beating and your blood would cease to circulate through your body? Silly right? You never give your blood flow a second thought. You just trust in the fact that it will keep on *performing its miracle* day after day after day, just as the air fills your lungs and the hair grows on your head. It's all about surrender and trusting that the Universe knows what It's doing. Right?

Well, that's exactly the same kind of trust and surrender that I am asking you to have when it comes to allowing God to flow through your life. The universe knows what She's doing. We *can* surrender our need to control It, *and just trust* in Its awesome power. The God force flows smoothly through everything. Our desire to control it only interferes with it. The power comes in letting go, not in holding on.

It's just like learning to ride a bicycle; the harder you fight for your balance the tougher it is. Suddenly, you just relax, *let go of your need to control it* and poof! You're balancing on two thin tires and riding around like you've been doing it your whole life. Heck, pretty soon you're even thinking about *letting go* and taking your hands off the handlebars—not for very long, just a second or two, just to see what might happen.

"Let go and let God." I first read those words on a bumper sticker pasted to the back of a dilapidated old station wagon as I raced past it, down the interstate—just outside Cincinnati Ohio—chasing what I thought was my dream. The year was 1983 and I was four years out of college, full of piss and vinegar and totally in charge—or so I thought—of my future. I knew what I wanted and I wasn't about to slow down or surrender to anyone or anything. Let go and let God? You had to be kidding!

But as my life unfolded from that point, as I began to acquire the material things that I thought would make me happy, I found that I was never satisfied. My ego just kept demanding more and more and like a junkie I kept searching for more and more ways to feed it. I would no sooner get something but that I wanted something else; no sooner arrive at the summit before I began searching for another mountain to climb.

Once, just after I had purchased a gorgeous new home on a golf course with a panoramic view of the Pacific ocean and just three blocks from the beach, I immediately began plotting how I could sell that home in six months and buy another one—a bigger one—a better one—not three blocks from the beach but right smack dab *on* the beach! Yeah! Then I'll be happy!

I never paused even once to enjoy the moment or give thanks for the gifts that had been bestowed upon me. I just kept *driving through* life, making things happen, always heading for that greener pasture—that *something better*—a little further down the road. With an ego that was now severely out of control, I blazed a trail by pushing hard and taking the bull by the horns. But taking a bull by the horns can be a very dangerous thing to do.

It took a while—make that a *very long time*—for the truth to sink in, but eventually I realized that I could *never find meaning in the meaningless*. It suddenly dawned on me that believing my life was a *do it yourself project*—that I could somehow make it on my own—was leading me nowhere fast; down the wrong road, further and further away from the happiness I desired.

That's when I allowed the God force within—the power I had let lie dormant—to come into my life and work along side of me. That's when I replaced fear with love and began to trust in something I couldn't see.

That's when I stopped fighting God, fired my ego and surrendered to spirit. That's when I began to *walk* the path of light.

The changes my life went through from that moment forward can best be described as nothing short of unbelievable! I rediscovered my highest gift, and began to follow my heart. I learned to be still and to listen to the voice within. The power of Spirit filled the void in my soul and I began to trust in the power of love. Suddenly the world seemed fresh and new. I had been reborn!

But here's the point: I had very little do with it. I just surrendered to the power of love and kept my focus on that power. It hasn't always been a bed of roses but now I know where to go to regain my balance and get back to center. Now I know that God lives within me and is available anytime, anywhere. I have found a strong spiritual foundation and what can only be called, *heaven on earth*.

Our lives begin to take on a new direction the minute we give our ego the boot. What we once thought were our dreams and desires no longer seem to fit. Suddenly, we develop a whole new sense of what it means to be happy. No longer do we feel that we must acquire things to feel worthy. We begin to accept the world and ourselves just as it is, just as we are. Peace begins to fill the void in our heart like a warm running fountain that keeps us in a perpetual state of bliss. Suddenly, we're in the flow of life riding the wave of creation instead of doing the doggy paddle and fighting the tide.

Oh, and you want to know something funny? We seem to think that if we get rid of our ego everything in our lives will fall apart. But I have found just the opposite to be true: Once we get rid of our ego, everything in life begins to come together. After the ego says, "adios," all that is left is love. Suddenly, surrendering to love becomes the only natural thing to do. But here's the catch: You can never see this when the ego is running the show. It's only after its departure that the truth appears. Again, it's all about surrender. You have to trust and surrender to the power of love if you want to move to a higher energy level and transcend the warped reality that the ego wants you to linger in.

At first, it's a little like walking around with a blindfold on because you're never quite sure where God is leading you. But soon, you become comfortable with the unknowing and lose your desire to look too far into the future. In what Zen terminology calls *satori*, you have an *instant awakening* where you begin to understand that the present moment is *the only thing you can really own*. Anything other than what's happening right here—right now—is simply seen as an illusion. You begin to enjoy the journey. Results no longer matter.

And that's probably the toughest thing about surrendering to the God force; releasing the egos need for results. We tend to want to focus on what something will *do for us* or what the outcome will be *versus just relaxing in the moment* and enjoying the *doing* itself. However, happiness lies within us; wherever we go, it goes. The only reason we don't know it's there is because we're not focused on the present moment. Our minds are either way out in the future somewhere or thinking about what happened yesterday, last week, last year. Repeat after me: You can only be happy *right now*. Even if you plan to be happy in the future, by the time you get there it will have become *right now*. Right? The trick is to always live in the present.

By detaching ourselves from results, we begin to focus more intensely on *the now* and not worry so much about what will or will not be. This *shift in perception* frees us because by focusing only on the present there is nothing to regret and nothing to worry about. The past is over and the future has yet to come. Without regret, guilt or worry, only happiness prevails. Don't worry. Be happy. It's true!

I once learned this valuable lesson about the past and all that we regret, while sailing off the coast of San Diego. We were underway in twenty-knot winds, when I became aware of *the wake* created by the boat as it moved through the water. Being an avid sailor, I had noticed the wake on many occasions of course, but this time something seemed to click. I have come to trust that whenever I get that special little feeling, it's time to pause and take notice; a lesson is about to present itself.

At that moment, I realized that *the wake does not drive the boat*—the wake is merely a result of where the boat has been. Stop the boat and the wake stops. I know this revelation sounds a little goofy, but just like the vapor trail behind a jet, we often think that our past—our wake—is pushing us forward. But it's not. It's only what's been left behind. And what's been left behind serves no useful purpose other than to remind us of where we have been.

From that moment forward, I began to acknowledge that our past has nothing to do with where we are today or where we choose to go tomorrow. Our past can only make improving our lives more difficult because we begin to think that our past defines us; that what we have done or have been is who and what we are and who and what we must continue to be. But our past cannot drive our future for *every day begins anew* with a fresh opportunity to move in the direction of our highest gift and live our life purpose. I let my past, with all its regrets and guilt, depart my life forever and surrendered to the only thing that can move us forward, the power of God.

Surrendering to the power within—the power of God—is not something that must be *believed* but rather is something that must be *known*. Surrendering is something that must be experienced and performed by the seeker. Surrendering to Spirit requires far more than simply choosing to *believe* in the stories and experiences of others, you *must know the truth* for yourself. It can't be lived through the autobiography of others any more than a kiss can be experienced by watching someone else do it.

It is, in this way, that surrendering to love becomes a *spiritual awakening*; void of any need for religious mandate. Surrender has no protocol, no prerequisites, and no rituals. Each step down the path—and even the pathway itself—is a personal connection to Spirit that can be as unique as the individual making the journey. In fact, often we resist to just surrender and walk the path of light because we don't want to follow the rules laid down by others. We want to connect to Spirit but the religious rules often push us away.

But eliminate the rules and you eliminate the resistance. There in lies the difference between what is religious and what is spiritual. The one-on-one connection to Spirit that can often be so difficult to find in the ritualized world of religion, unfolds like an open book in the *all-accepting realm* of spirituality. Suddenly, we're free to let our heart fall a little further down our sleeve. We feel comfortable dropping all pretenses and begin to hang out with God just as we would an old friend. Our relationship with God begins to take on a welcomed casualness that feels like a well-worn pair of jeans.

At this new level of awareness, the God force becomes something *we can trust in* because it is something we *know*. We have lived *It,* breathed *It* and allowed *It* to be felt deep within our souls. Fear subsides and love prevails. We begin to *follow our own truth* and allow our sixth sense and intuition—gifts from God—to lead us in every brave endeavor. Feelings take precedent over logic as we develop an inner *knowing that transcends understanding.* Making decisions becomes easy because we begin to trust what we feel and follow the direction of our heart. We already know the answer, for we *are* the answer. We have surrendered to the power within and begin to use it to light the world.

A Course In Miracles teaches: "Nothing real can be threatened. Nothing unreal exists. Herein lies the peace of God." Since nothing can be threatened, only peace exists. Anything other than peace is but an illusion played out in our minds. Anything that is not peaceful—war, hatred, anger, violence—is nonexistent *unless we choose to give these things life* by giving them our thoughts. What we think about expands. As we think, so we become. Think only peace and love and that is all you will ever know. As *The Course* teaches, that is all you need to know.

The pathways that lead to surrender—to God—are like spokes in a wheel. Each connects to the center but from entirely different directions. And so it is that we must embrace through tolerance and understanding, the pathways chosen by those who differ from us. We must respect the different spokes on the wheel and allow other souls to connect to God without any interference or lack of acceptance on our part. We must simply surrender and allow love—the universal power that unites us all—to lead us to the presence of God. We must embrace the freedom to make that connection any way we choose, and allow others the freedom to do the same.

So let me ask you again: Would you like to experience heaven on earth? Would you like to get rid of all the unhappiness in your life and experience only joy? Does the idea of living a blissful existence, unencumbered by the weight of grief and sorrow appeal to you? Or, how about never having to worry about anything ever again? Does that sound good? Would you like a little of that?

All of this can be yours in the instant it takes to surrender and let the God force direct your life. In the time it takes to complain—one more time—about all that is wrong with your world, you can make the choice to set yourself free. Life was never meant to be a struggle. Believe it. Act upon it. And allow the miracles of the Universe to unfold before your very eyes.

Some Things To Consider

How much time do you spend trying to control the elements of your world with only the direction of your mind? Try a little experiment. Spend an entire week taking your hands off the handlebars and just let the Universe lead you instead of the other way around. See if you can allow your ego to take a backseat to your soul for a change. Allow yourself to just "feel" your way through the day and begin to notice the so-called coincidences in your life. After a week of doing this, (hey, it's only a week!) note if you feel any differently about your ability to let go and let Go(d).

ABOUT THE AUTHOR

Jeffrey Alan Hall is an author, lecturer and spiritual Life Coach. He is the founder of **Soulworks**® Life Coaching and **Souls@Work**® workshops and seminars. Dedicated to unleashing the full potential of the human spirit, Jeffrey works with both individuals and organizations, inspiring others to find their life purpose and become their highest gift. He lives with his family in Evergreen, Colorado.

Jeffrey enjoys hearing from his readers and can be reached at his web site: www.soul-works.net or 1-800-495-SOUL

0-595-21027-9